SEVEN PILLARS for Life and KINGDOM PROSPERITY

DR. ALAN PATEMAN

SEVEN PILLARS for Life and KINGDOM PROSPERITY

BOOK TITLE:
Seven Pillars for Life and Kingdom Prosperity

This book first published in 2016; second edition in 2025

Published by APMI Publications
In Partnership with Truth for the Journey Books **17**
P.O. Box 17,
55051 Barga (LU),
Italy

Email: publications@alanpatemanworldmissions.com
www.AlanPatemanWorldMissions.com

APMI Publications and Truth for the Journey Books are a division of Alan Pateman World Missions

Printed in the United States of America, Europe and Asia

Paperback ISBN: 978-1-909132-46-7
Hardcover ISBN: 978-1-909132-94-8
eBook ISBN: 978-1-909132-47-4

Acknowledgements:
Author/Design/Senior Editor/Publisher: Apostle Dr. Alan Pateman
Editing/Proofreading/Research: Dr. Jennifer Pateman
Computer Administration/Office Manager: Dr. Dorothea Struhlik
Cover Image Credit: © Anna Om, © Andrey Kuzmin, © Eky Chan, www.fotolia.com

Unless otherwise indicated, all scriptural quotations are from the HOLY BIBLE, NEW INTERNATIONAL VERSION ®. NIV ®. Copyright © 1973, 1978, 1984 by the International Bible Society. Used by permission of Zondervan Publishing House. All rights reserved.

Where scriptures appear with special emphasis (in bold, italic or underlined) we have edited them ourselves in order to bring focused attention within the context of this subject being taught.

❖

Dedication

I dedicate this book to my son
Andrew James Pateman

You are diligent, handsome, strong and wise.
Your laughter and wit fill the house.
Your talent in art is extreme.
Son, I am so proud of you.
Love you forever.

❖

Table of Contents

❖

Acknowledgements

I want to thank all of my friends and colleagues who have endorsed this book by contributing to its publication. Your selfless support is truly admirable. I appreciate each and everyone of you, your families, ministries and churches.

In particular I would like to mention Apostle George and Pastor Stella Hooper from Lifegate Christian Ministries International in Liverpool England, Pastors Tony Ejiugwo and Felicia Achazie from Reconciliation Ministries International in Poggibonsi Italy, Elder Bright and Mrs. Olafunke Dzikunu from Church of Pentecost in Parma Italy, Pastor Isaac Edomwonyi from Christ Intervention Ministries in Pistoia Italy and Rev. Blessing Ogbonmwan from Christ Apostolic Church of God Mission in Merksem Belgium.

❖

Introduction

In over thirty years of ministry, it's true to say that I have seen much in the way of success and failure, within my own Christian walk and the Body of Christ at large. Including witnessing and in some cases being a part of, the many different streams and theological approaches to the same gospel truth, that's taught from many different angles; throughout both denominational and non-denominational structures.

We must ask, "What causes the Body of Christ, Christians then, to walk the walk of success?" In the process of trying to answer this question, I felt it important or necessary to put together a number of pillars, which we can all harness and employ, that have helped me within my own Christian walk.

The fact of the matter is this; we can't minister out of an unreality. We can only minister out of success.

Traditions are one thing, but a revelation of the Father's love, along with an understanding that not only does He want us to have a personal relationship with Him, but also for us to have success and overcome in this life, in order to fulfil His divine purposes and plans for which we were created.

Therefore I submit these **"Seven Pillars for Life and Kingdom Prosperity"** to you, because it's my desire that you walk in the triumphs that God has ordained for you. This book is a compilation and consolidation of many other materials, which I have taught from over the years.

I pray that you are inspired to walk in the success that God has specifically mapped out for you.

Dr Alan Pateman

First Pillar

LOVE

❖

CHAPTER 1

His Unfailing Love

L et's jump straight in at the most foundational pillar for *Life and Kingdom Prosperity*, which of course is love. What other motive is there for life? In fact there are many other ingredients in life but as God's chosen, love really ought to be the beginning of every step we take!

In the Greek language and in its simplest form, **agape** is pure *(or divine)*, selfless, sacrificial and unconditional. Which perfectly describes the highest of the four types of love found in scripture; the type that Jesus had for His Father and for His disciples *(John 15:9-10)*. God the Father on the other hand demonstrated *agape* by sending His Son Jesus to die on the cross for us. Ultimately *agape* was His chiefest motive and Jesus was His choicest gift!

*For God **loved** the world so much **that he gave** his one and only Son, so that everyone who believes in him will not perish but have eternal life.*

(John 3:16 NLT)

Love endures long and is patient and kind; love never is envious nor boils over with jealousy, is not boastful or vainglorious, does not display itself haughtily. It is not conceited (arrogant and inflated with pride); it is not rude (unmannerly) and does not act unbecomingly.

***Love (God's love in us)** does not insist on its own rights or its own way, for it is not self-seeking; it is not touchy or fretful or resentful; it takes no account of the evil done to it [it pays no attention to a suffered wrong]. It does not rejoice at injustice and unrighteousness, but rejoices when right and truth prevail.*

Love bears up under anything and everything that comes, is ever ready to believe the best of every person, its hopes are fadeless under all circumstances, and it endures everything [without weakening].

(1 Corinthians 13:4-7 AMP)

Love Offers Itself

We in turn can love God. To love God fully means to lay down one's life and live completely for Him. In the same way that He completely gave Jesus, we must completely give ourselves to Him. Although this does *not* involve us going to the cross *again* to die a physical death, it does involve some spiritual *dying to self.* However in comparison with what Christ gave up, we experience more gain than loss, in every aspect of life. He became poor that we might become rich!

However there is an extra clause here. As God, "so loves us," we in turn are obligated to, "love others." Allowing His *agape* love to overflow from us, to all the people of the world *(1 John 4:21)*.

This type of *(divine)* love that we are discussing here is not a soppy, mushy kind of love. Rather it is direct, forceful at times and demonstrates the very power of God. In other words we too must love with power – His power. Not waiting for people to come to us, but reaching out to them and meeting them with this dynamic love of Christ; a love that procrastinates *not* but always acts now, **"...here am I; send me"** *(Isaiah 6:8)*.

Love Demonstrates the Power of God

There are millions of people crying out for God, it is our commission and responsibility to reach them. Not in a religious way but in a way that people can see that we mean what we say! People will never be interested in what we say, until they see *(with evidence)* how much we CARE! We must demonstrate our love, not just mouth it! Just as God demonstrated His love through Christ, we too must demonstrate His love through us. **Actions always speak louder than words!**

In fact scripture teaches us to give ourselves to one another in love, meeting each other's needs. Not a demanding love, but one that is freely given and received, no conditions or strings attached! We must not be afraid to love forcefully; we must fearlessly demonstrate our love and God's love for people.

The following parable of "The Good Samaritan," fully exhibits this kind of demonstrated love, which is not by mere choice but command!

On one occasion an expert in the law stood up to test Jesus. "Teacher," he asked, "what must I do to inherit eternal life?" "What is written in the Law?" He replied. "How do you read it?" He answered, **"'Love the Lord your God with all your heart and with all your soul and with all your strength and with all your mind;' and, 'Love your neighbour as yourself.'"** "You have answered correctly," Jesus replied. "Do this and you will live."

Nevertheless in an attempt to justify himself, he asked Jesus, "And who is my neighbour?" In reply Jesus said: "A man was going down from Jerusalem to Jericho, when he was attacked by robbers. They stripped him of his clothes, beat him and went away, leaving him half dead. A priest happened to be going down the same road, and when he saw the man, he passed by on the other side. So too, a Levite, when he came to the place and saw him, passed by on the other side.

Love is Responsible not Emotional

A Samaritan, as he travelled, came where the man was; and when he saw him, he took pity on him. He went to him and bandaged his wounds, pouring on oil and wine. Then he put the man on his own donkey, brought him to an Inn and took care of him. The next day he took out two denarii and gave them to the innkeeper. 'Look after him,' he said, 'and when I return, I will reimburse you for any extra expense you may have.'"

"Which of these three do you think was a neighbour to the man who fell into the hands of robbers?" The expert in the law replied, "The one who had mercy on him." Jesus told him, "Go and do likewise" *(Luke 10:25-37)*.

More than a Gesture

Mercy is an *action* not just a *feeling (of mere empathy or identification)* and this neighbourly-kind-of-love that Jesus requires of us, is responsible rather than emotional. It is STRONG-ACTION-TAKING-LOVE.

The Samaritan did not become emotional, but took responsibility instead. There is a BIG difference. He demonstrated love and did not just sympathise with it!

It would have been *an-act-of-love-undone* had the Good Samaritan failed the troubled traveller by offering him the gesture of his prayers only.

While there is always room for discretion, there is also room for powerful and confrontational love. The world needs this kind of love. Not a compromising and religious kind but a strong love that looks to solve and to fix. In addition, strong godly love is always willing to confront and expose sin, only however, so that change can take place, via conviction and not condemnation. God loves us too much to leave us the way that we are! This bold, active and Godly type of love - is particularly characteristic of the apostolic and prophetic Church.

Jesus Moved with Compassion

What was it that Jesus *saw* that moved or triggered His compassion? And what do we *see*? If there's no compassion – there's no love!

Jesus had compassion on them and touched their eyes.
Immediately they received their sight and followed him.
(Matthew 20:34 KJV)

It's a genuine question: what do we *see* when we look at people? Do we see what God sees or do we only see their faults? Only seeing other people's faults make us harsh and judgmental. Conversely if we are willing to see on the other side of their faults, so that we can discern their real needs, this is when we can develop genuine compassion! There is a BIG difference between judgment and compassion! Therefore we must see what Jesus sees in people, so that we can operate in the same compassion that He did.

Empathy

A well-known evangelist Kathryn Kuhlman once said, *"You can never get rid of your own troubles unless you take upon yourself the troubles of others."* Some would call this empathy by the Spirit of God. Empathy means: stepping into the shoes of others, to feel what they feel. Empathy identifies with others on a much deeper level than sympathy.

This could create a major imbalance of course – if taken to the extreme. But like Joyce Meyer often encourages those in her audiences *(those who might be habitually complaining about their lives)* to go and spend a day in a local hospital or care centre, to sit and talk with those who have lost limbs or who are resigned to wheel chairs for the rest of their lives. She rightly points out, that such a simple step can radically alter a habitual complainer, by helping them create a better perspective!

Seeing what others go through can quickly inspire right thinking in our own lives! And in this context empathy is a good thing to pursue. But taken to its unhealthy extreme, empathy can depress and oppress you if you live in other people's shoes all the time!

Compassion however can involve receiving certain burdens from the Lord, but is something entirely different from depression! Because if genuine, the burden will "lift" only to come back again when the Holy Spirit is ready to inspire us to pray or act in some specific way.

Love must be Consistent to be Authentic

The moral of the story is this: without the Holy Spirit even our best attempts at being compassionate are useless! Only He can trigger the right emotions or responses in us. To summarise: true compassion is like the anointing, it will come for a purpose and then lift again; everything has a purpose in the Kingdom of God. It's a divine trigger and works closely with intercession.

Paul tells us in Colossians 3:12-15 *(AMP)* to clothe ourselves with *(actively put on)* compassion:

Clothe yourselves therefore, as God's own chosen ones (His own picked representatives), [who are] purified and holy and well-beloved [by God Himself, by putting on behaviour marked by] **tender hearted pity and mercy, kind feeling,** *a lowly opinion of yourselves, gentle ways, [and] patience [which is tireless and long-suffering, and has the power to endure whatever comes, with good temper].*

Be gentle and forbearing with one another and, if one has a difference (a grievance or complaint) against another, readily pardoning each other; even as the Lord has [freely] forgiven you, so must you also [forgive]. And above all these [put on] love and enfold yourselves with the bond of perfectness [which binds everything together completely in ideal harmony].

And let the peace (soul harmony which comes) from Christ rule (act as umpire continually) in your hearts [deciding and settling with finality all questions that arise in your minds, in that peaceful state] to which as [members of Christ's] one body you were also called [to live]. And be thankful (appreciative), [giving praise to God always].

As Jesus Himself moved with this kind of compassion we too must have this divine heart for those people that God brings our way for help. For instance when I am ministering I am totally aware of the fact that I need to have love and compassion if I am ever going to be used by God to help bring about the kind of "break-through" that people need in their lives. I can never afford to have a judgmental attitude whether in the pulpit or out of it. **Love must be consistent to be authentic.**

Counterfeit Love will always Sympathise

However there is always the counterfeit. Sympathy in the correct context can be healthy and has a legitimate role to play. On the other hand, sympathy can also be nothing more than *perverted love*. By this I mean that sympathy can be very convincing and quite seductive, tempting us to sympathize with people or circumstances, even at the expense of grieving the Holy Spirit. In this context, when sympathy works in direct conflict with God's Spirit and purposes, it is corrupt. Sympathy will generally get us to focus on our emotions rather than obedience.

For example sympathy has lead most of us into the positions/conditions that we find ourselves in today. We have been sympathetically patted on the back and told, "There, there... things will get better," but never shown how to take responsibility and get out of our distress! We don't need to be duped or convinced to stay in bondage, **what we need is love's liberating and redemptive role in our lives, that always looks to restore.**

❖

CHAPTER 2

The Fellowship of Love

The last verse of 2 Corinthians is a powerful one and the Amplified Version puts it like this: "The grace *(favor and spiritual blessing)* of the Lord Jesus Christ and the love of God and the **presence and fellowship** *(the communion and sharing together, and participation)* in the Holy Spirit be with you all."

> *The grace of the Lord Jesus Christ, and the love of God, and the fellowship of the Holy Spirit, [is] with you all! Amen.*
>
> *(2 Corinthians 13:14 YLT)*

Everything in this verse points to a three-fold companionship with God. Remembering that one of His names is also **"Emmanuel"** which means **"God with us."** This is reflected in the Young's Literal Translation above where it says "...the Holy Spirit [is] with you all!" All three Persons of the Godhead: Father, Son and Holy Spirit, are active in providing this companionship. The Father brings *love*. Jesus brings *grace* and both, love and grace are so potent that they can only originate from God *(Ephesians 2:8; John 3:16)*.

His grace allows us entry into this divine companionship, while His love keeps it breathing and vibrant. However the Holy Spirit also plays a vital role in nurturing and cultivating this divine companionship - and it's His contribution to the relationship that we focus on in this chapter.

Fellowship Involves Joint Participation

We begin by looking into the Greek meaning for the word *fellowship* used in 2 Corinthians 13:14. This Greek word is **koinonia:** *communion, communication, contribution, distribution,* **joint participation** *and* **intimacy.**

So we can describe our fellowship with the Holy Spirit as something that is divinely intimate and involves joint participation! However it also involves words like **partnership,** *(social) intercourse and (pecuniary or economic) benefaction* - coming from the closely related word *skoinonos and koinos* meaning: *sharer, i.e. associate: - companion, fellowship, partaker,* **partner** *(see Strong's #G2844; #G2839).*

So as we can see this Greek word for fellowship *(koinonia)* is a complex, rich, and thoroughly fascinating Greek approach to building community and teamwork. It has such a multitude of meanings that no single English word is adequate to express its depth and richness. Therefore however we look at this word, we can derive so much from it in order to help us decipher what is exactly meant by fellowship with the Holy Spirit.

Joint Participation

First of all let's break this up slightly for easier grasp – as *koinonia* has superb applications.

Let's start here by saying that fellowship of the Holy Spirit is not a one-way street! It is a sharing of wills, feelings, and knowledge. We share what we have or know with Him and He shares what He has and knows with us! Jesus said, "He will tell you whatever He hears [from the Father; He will give the message that has been given to Him], and He will announce and declare to you the things that are to come [that will happen in the future].

He will honour and glorify Me because He will take of *(receive, draw upon)* what is Mine and will reveal *(declare, disclose, transmit)* it to you" *(John 16:13b-14 AMP)*.

Just think, He knows the secrets of heaven and is willing to reveal such to all who are willing to "jointly participate" with Him. The Holy Spirit has direct access to the Father's loving heart, which means whatever the Father speaks, He hears and is able to communicate that with us! In other words we can enjoy *insider* information if we will be vulnerable enough to abandon our fears and draw closer to Him, as James encourages here:

Come close to the one true God, and **He will draw close to you.**

(James 4:8 VOICE)

The original Greek here for "draw nigh" or "come close" depending on what translation of the bible you have - literally means: "approach" or "be at hand" for Him. Once we approach God like this or make ourselves available, then He can reciprocate with His presence!

Intimate Availability

What an awesome reality this is, to have God Almighty close by and always "at hand." Can we fathom the beautiful implications of this and the impact that such loving commitment and fellowship can have on our everyday lives?

Notice that verse 8 in James chapter 4 stipulates that we must "come close" or "draw close" first. This prerequisite or condition plainly puts the onus and responsibility on us, which means that the quality, quantity and regularity of the fellowship that we share with the Holy Spirit largely rests on our willingness to make ourselves *available.*

Yet what may seem like a precondition is only really a response to what God has already done for us and initiated through Christ. For example 1 John 4:19 confirms: "We love because he **first** loved us..." meaning that God was the catalyst not us! It was God who first initiated the relationship - not us! The only reason that we can *come close* or make ourselves available to Him at all is because Jesus was first made available to us.

Our ability to fellowship with God, started with Him. However in terms of a relationship being a two-way-street, then our willingness in the response will always be a prerequisite.

Potent Partnership

Through Him we can face any challenge that life throws at us. And within this divine relationship that we share with Him, where fellowship is intimate, we are able to communicate our most personal issues, whether joyful desires or concerns of the heart. It's fellowship that enjoys spontaneity and freedom rather than just dull monologue!

In this respect we should always freely accommodate the Holy Spirit into our lives; appreciating, respecting, adoring and fully recognising Him in everything that we do.

The type of fellowship that we are discussing here in this particular chapter - represents a most effective and potent partnership! All partnerships exist to enhance growth, productivity and profit. Partners strategize *(manage)* together and share in all successes and failures. However when we consider fellowship with the Holy Spirit in this way, then we must always recognise Him as the Senior Partner *simply because He brings so much more to the table than we do, the very purposes of God!*

For example consider the infinite resources and knowledge that He possesses; which can only make His strategies and methods perfect and above reproach! In addition, regard the fact that no matter how much He outranks everyone, He still leaves room for us to be heard!

Trusted Strategist

Also the Holy Spirit is a major strategist. He navigates for us - if we allow ourselves to be led – and His GPS never fails! When He strategizes on our behalf, this ensures superior results. We owe it to ourselves to be consistently available to fellowship with Him, even when it's routinely inconvenient! Only then can He reveal heaven's intricate purposes to our spirits, how He plans to unfold them and most importantly where our cooperation is required.

That place of fellowship allows the Holy Spirit to debrief and inject us with vital information and clear instruction. So we can down load and digest pieces of divine blueprint, so that no future plans or efforts will be jeopardized.

We must always *live ready* to listen to His instruction and willing to receive His help for the follow-through of that instruction! The best fact of all is that He not only lends us His expertise but also His power!

Even though partners share victories - the credit must all be His! He is unable to fail and neither will we if we learn to follow and yield in the manner that we are discussing here. It is elementary then that in the degree to which we *cooperate* is the same degree to which we will succeed.

Active, Productive and Meaningful

Everything the Holy Spirit does is to empower us. Therefore we can be certain that regular fellowship with Him only benefits our lives. Heaven's intentions can then be realised. It is through deep fellowship like this that history can be changed as a result! Not sitting in a lotus position meditating and chanting in tongues which is not fellowship but religious ritual that some might like to call fellowship! True fellowship with the Holy Spirit is not static or stagnant but the most active and productive part of our daily lives.

He talks with us "on the go!" Nothing restricts Him. Not time or space! He is always ready for us to plug in and enjoy this vital living-connection with Him; such connectedness should never be fragmented. For example we should never spend our Christian lives *travelling-in-and-out-of-His-presence* but rather *live* there!

Sensitive Accountability

In fact the kind of "fellowship" we discuss here is very accountable simply because the Holy Spirit specialises in transforming the written instruction of God's Word into practical application in our everyday lives. Therefore it is vital that we learn to partner with Him on every level; being open to His input and advice *before* making decisions.

I'm not suggesting that we need the Holy Spirit to tell us when to clean our teeth - some things we can work out for ourselves! When to wash and to eat etc., He gives us enough credit to do that sort of thing on our own! However when it comes to the larger decisions of life, it must become an established discipline, to pass things with Him first. It takes time but we must pursue such a discipline, especially when the end product of living in such a way has the potential to change our destiny or other people's lives.

Sensitivity to the Holy Spirit on this level means that He can depend on us to *act* in obedience no matter what the circumstances say. This is where we allow the unction of the Holy Spirit to dictate our thoughts rather than the conditions of the world around us.

Simple Acts of Obedience

Plus we can't underestimate the influence that our simple acts of obedience have on others - even if we deem such acts as insignificant - we can guarantee that when the Holy Spirit is in control - He always has others in mind and an agenda that pursues their freedom and liberty!

Now the Lord is that Spirit: and where the Spirit of the Lord is, there is liberty.
                                    (2 Corinthians 3:17)

It is important to add right now that the Holy Spirit does not promote the same *self-gratifying-life* that the world does, rather He demotes selfishness and promotes self-*less*-ness instead. He is not our spiritual maid who picks up the pieces that we leave behind or our PR-Guru who manages all our damage-control issues!

We live in a narcissistic generation that spends billions on the pursuit of happiness: pleasure seekers with an over inflated sense of importance, with their self-help-coaches getting rich from their clients weak and confused identity.

Not for Hire!

For this reason we must not merely identify the Holy Spirit as a *(divine)* personal-trainer. HE IS SO MUCH MORE! It is a danger to limit Him to such an earthly status.

Besides, He is not for hire *(paid-by-the-hour)*, He never closes-shop or leaves our side. He is ever available. He shares in our failures as much as our successes, so that the challenges of life don't overwhelm us. He works in us so that our spiritual instincts sufficiently evolve, to the point that we are more attuned to His overcoming nature than our own indulgent-self-pity.

The world around us is so overly obsessed with the god of self. Yet in Christ we learn that life is not all about self and that we don't exist just to rescue ourselves from any sense of difficulty! Instead we learn to overcome in ways that help others overcome as a result. In fact with His divine influence upon our lives, normal temptations should be more easily overcome, showcasing a genuine lifestyle of self-control and restraint that will be a valid witness to them.

Conviction is always Present

This is generally how we know if someone is truly walking with the Spirit of God or not - because if they really know Him *(and are known of Him)*, then the conviction of holiness is always present. This means that they will not feel well with themselves, in the presence of sin and will conscientiously work on adjusting themselves, in pursuit of maturity and self-control. Whereas those who are too comfortable around sin, are probably not walking too closely with the Holy Spirit at all!

For the sake of balance here and in the context of evangelism we cannot afford to be overly delicate about sin. It is then that we must be open to embrace those in the deepest sins without becoming one with their sin in the process. For example Galatians 6:1 *(GW)* says this, "...if a person gets trapped by wrongdoing, those of you who are spiritual should help that person turn away from doing wrong. Do it in a gentle way. At the same time watch yourself so that you also are not tempted."

To continue, one of the greatest chapters in the bible that describes this privileged partnership we have with the Holy Spirit, is Romans 8. The entire chapter is a treasure in fact, but verse 26 just says, "So too the Holy Spirit comes to our aid and bears us up in our weakness..." *(AMP)* What comfort this offers us? With the love of our Heavenly Father and the redemption work of Christ, coupled with the presence of the person of the Holy Spirit, who is ever "close at hand," we can confidently affirm such a privileged position by saying that truly all things, "work together for good for those who love God" *(verse 28).*

United Movement

This final application of *koinonia* is taken from another literal translation meaning: "moving together with..." We could say, "travelling together with," which can be seen in the context of our prayer lives. For instance He moves or travels with us *as* we pray, by "moving or transporting" our prayer from earth to heaven.

This is referenced in Romans 8:26. As usual the Amplified Version of the bible puts it more poignantly: "So too the [Holy] Spirit comes to our aid and bears us up in our weakness; for we do not know what prayer to offer nor how to offer it worthily as we ought, but the Spirit Himself **goes to meet our supplication** and pleads in our behalf with unspeakable yearnings and groanings too deep for utterance."

So with this better grasp of the word *fellowship* from 2 Corinthians 13:14, and by using its original meaning we can fully recognise that fellowship *(koinonia)* with the Holy Spirit represents one of life's greatest pillars.

It's a rich, living and loving partnership that intimately works together with Almighty God.

Second Pillar

PRAYER

❖

CHAPTER 3

God is Able

I n this second pillar for Life and Kingdom Prosperity we are going to begin looking at the subject of prayer.

"I have so much to do that I spend several hours in prayer before I am able to do it" (John Wesley).

"I have been driven many times to my knees by the overwhelming conviction that I had absolutely no other place to go" (Abraham Lincoln).

Once we discover that prayer isn't just for the few, it becomes obvious that whatever our station in life, we all need prayer.

In fact no measure of success or prosperity can ever take the place of divine intimacy, something that can only be found on our knees before the Lord.

"Do you know what prayer is? It is not begging God for this and that. The first thing we have to do is to get you beggars to quit begging until a little faith moves in your souls" (John G. Lake).

Let fresh revelation flood your heart and rebirth the desire and urgency for prayer, as you once knew it in the beginning of your walk with the Lord. No matter who we are, the cares of this world seek to crowd God out of our lives. This alone makes prayer a discipline not a recreation!

It all starts with Relationship

Although, having said that, the most basic element of prayer is *relationship.* That is the essential starting point, from which all other types of prayer proceeds. A rich and intimate relationship with God, not unlike what E.M Bounds was referring to when he said, "Those who know God the best are the richest and most powerful in prayer. Little acquaintance with God, strangeness and coldness to Him, make prayer a rare and feeble thing."

Yet even the seemingly successful ministers of today, who preach regularly in their own pulpits, admit lacking a decent prayer life! E.M Bounds would rightly comment on this phenomenon by saying, "The Church is looking for better methods; God is looking for better men. The Holy Ghost does not flow through methods, but through men. He does not come on machinery, but on men. He does not anoint plans, but men... men of prayer."

With this in mind it definitely seems to me that just about everything in life is designed to take us away from praying.

Not least modern technology! Take the latest devices and gadgets we like to own, such as the iPhone or iPad for example! While they are great tools-for-the-job it has become way too easy turning them on first thing in the morning or last thing at night. We even take them to bed with us for that last minute *fix* before we close our eyes!

It can be days or even weeks before we realise that our *intimacy* with the Lord is missing, through neglect of His Word and lost opportunities in His presence.

The hope is, that the void which builds up within us as a result, eventually stops us in our tracks and that the conviction of the Holy Spirit, arrests us and brings us back to that place of prayer and intimacy. Where unhindered and unpretentious worship flows and where our inner-man feels most at home!

Then Comes the Responsibility

To continue, besides this personal and relational aspect of praying, the responsibility of prayer is not neglected. However I want to clarify here that neither is prayer *(intercession)* just an elitist ministry for the few! We are all initiates! And it certainly is not a secret society just for self-confessing-martyrs and depressed burden bearers!

Every believer has the right and the calling to stand in the gap for others. With a lifestyle that's consistent so that when the opportunity arises and the need beckons, they are ready to pray. Such a readiness can only be developed into a person's life that intercedes continually.

I urge, then, first of all, that requests, prayers, intercession and thanksgiving be made for everyone – for kings and all those in authority, that we may live peaceful and quiet lives in all godliness and holiness. This is good, and pleases God our Savior, who wants all men to be saved and to come to a knowledge of the truth. For there is one God and one mediator between God and men, the man Christ Jesus.

(1 Timothy 2:1-5)

We must be skilled intercessors, as Spurgeon well pointed out, "There is a general kind of praying which fails for lack of precision. It is as if a regiment of soldiers should all fire off their guns anywhere. Possibly somebody would be killed, but the majority of the enemy would be missed" *(Charles H. Spurgeon)*. This takes knowledge of the Word and how to rightly *divide* it. Jesus used it expressly in the wilderness to fight Satan; so must we *(2 Timothy 2:15; Matthew 4:10)*.

Are You Willing?

He sees that there's no one to help. He's astounded that there's no one to intercede. So with his own power he wins a victory. His righteousness supports him.

(Isaiah 59:16 GW)

Because of its vastness we cannot possibly cover every aspect of prayer in one or two chapters, it will require both patience and time to get through it all! So we will take one step at a time and will begin with "are you willing?"

Intercession is just one part of prayer, which is a world of study and activity in itself. Not just relational, as we brought out already. Rather intercession is the part of all praying that is much weightier and holds much more responsibility. A task that we are ALL expected to engage in.

So why is intercession a weightier realm of prayer? Simply because there is more spiritual involvement, in other words there is more fervency and feeling in the spirit. Our spirit is more involved in intercession than in ordinary prayers and there is a continuous burden until the prayer is answered.

The Need for Prayer is a Mystery

In addition God still actively seeks intercessors today, "I sought for a man among them, that should make up the hedge, and stand in the gap before me for the land, that I should not destroy it: but I found none" *(Ezekiel 22:30 KJV)*. There is a real mystery as to why God still needs our prayers and why it is a force to be reckoned with; that breaks the power of evil and releases the plans and purposes of God on the earth.

> *This is how you should pray: Our Father in heaven, let your name be kept holy.* **Let your kingdom come. Let your will be done on earth as it is done in heaven.**
> *(Matthew 6:9-10 GW)*

Even in today's world, we know that prayer does not lack any power, "The earnest *(heartfelt, continued)* prayer of a righteous man **makes tremendous power available [dynamic in its working]**" *(James 5:16 AMP - see also Ephesians 6:18; James 4:7-8)*.

So what stops us? Why the denial, spiritual apathy and laziness? We have all had to face this and fight our own lack of willingness where prayer was concerned, even when thoroughly convinced of its effectiveness. This defies logic. Still we experience on a daily basis this challenge *not* to pray! **Yet our enemy is often much more aware than we are, of just how effective it really is!**

> *From the time of John the Baptizer until now, the kingdom of heaven has been forcefully **advancing**, and forceful people have been **seizing it**.*
>
> *(Matthew 11:12 GW)*

Wondrous Responsibility and Power

Andrew Murray in his book, "The Ministry of Intercession," laid a real challenge at our doorstep, both for individuals and the Body of Jesus Christ at large. He wrote, "There is a world with its needs entirely dependent on and waiting to be helped by intercession; there is a God in heaven with His all-sufficient supply for all those needs, waiting to be asked; there is a Church with its wondrous calling and its surprises, **waiting to be roused to a sense of its wondrous responsibility and power**" (Murray 170). See also Proverbs 31:8-9 KJV.

So with all this power in our hands, the perfect remedy to all our ills and pains, why do we still lack the *willingness to pray? (So evident at the local prayer meeting when so few volunteer!)* Why was it that even God Himself could not find anyone to intercede?

This is a genuine phenomena, but certainly not unique to our modern experience. It has been true throughout Church history *(except during revivals),* that even with so much power and influence readily at hand, we still shy away from the very thing that has the potential to change history forever!

Much is Required

There is nothing passive about prayer and it requires much from us. It is certainly not as simple as just *asking-n-getting* like a microwave transaction! No! It takes much more diligence and staying power before any break-through is realised. Considerable valuable time, thought and energy are required. Yet anyone who is given to prayer will testify the results far outweigh the costs!

Conversely those who are still subject to their fallen nature and the flesh will not easily be given to anything that requires the slightest bit of self-sacrifice! But we are not discussing them. We talk of the prayers of the redeemed; those who know the call to prayer; know its power and objective but still opt out!

If prayer requires much, haven't we been given so much more? Perhaps this is better handled in the old English of the King James: **"...unto whomsoever much is given, of him shall be much required:** and to whom men have committed much, of him they will ask the more" *(Luke 12:48 KJV).*

Together let us meet this call to prayer - so that when God looks for intercessors – He finds them! Let us discover together what this mystery called prayer is all about and may we discover a new found willingness to pray that we have never encountered before. A desire to stand in the gap on a level that we have not experienced before; as the Holy Spirit stirs us up to face our most holy responsibility.

God is Obligated to His own Words

Judgment without mercy will be shown to anyone who has not been merciful. **Mercy triumphs over judgment.**
(James 2:13)

Let's continue. In the last few paragraphs we discussed our own willingness towards prayer. Now we move on to discuss God's willingness. **Yes! He is more willing to answer our prayers than we are willing to pray!** We never have to spend hours in vain babbling trying to get God's attention, twisting His arm, manipulating or trying to convince Him of His own will! **For if we pray according to His Word, He is already obligated to answer. He cannot refute His own Words!**

The Logos; God's *written* Word, that's now in leather bound covers with golden edges rather than wooden scrolls, is what we use when we pray. **It is our plumb line and we only get off-centre when trying to negotiate the terms of His will, against our own!**

So is God willing? Yes He is! But consider this. Most folks don't ever struggle with the fact that God is *able* but always need convincing that He's *willing*. For example, if you asked a random person in the street, *"Can* God heal?" Most would answer, "Yes!" If instead you asked, *"Will* God heal?" most would answer, "I don't know!"

As Willing as He is Able

This is not an indictment against His *ability* but against His *will*. It's logic after all. God almighty should be *able* to do anything. But we're not so certain He will *"...for me?"*

That's where the devil's in the detail. It's not a problem for us to believe God can, but if we think somehow that we're not good enough, that's what causes the problem.

Once we have it settled in our hearts and minds that **God is *as willing as He is able* to perform His Word,** the struggle automatically stops. Now it is we who must be willing, to believe and to receive! The blockage does not exist with God; it is with us! *(Note: sin also creates a blockage between God and man - but that is another subject!)*

So how then can we be so sure that God *wants* to heal? The written Word reveals it to be so. Jesus used the authority of the written Word during His stint in the wilderness! Notice how both Jesus and His opponent *(the devil)* knew exactly what was written! The only difference was that Satan wrongly divided God's Word, while Jesus rightly divided it! BIG DIFFERENCE! One effective and powerful the other twisted and out of context. Demonstrating to us that **if we put the same rightly divided Word in our mouths, it will have just as much power to defeat Satan as it did in the mouth of Jesus!** *(2 Timothy 2:15)*

If God delights in mercy that triumphs over judgment, what on earth does that actually mean? In short – God loves to be merciful but demands that we also show mercy; we achieve this not only through our actions but also through our prayers.

Why is He Holding Back?

Andrew Murray in his book called, "The Ministry of Intercession" in chapter 14 wrote the following: "Here is a God of glory able to meet all these needs. We are told that He delights in mercy that He waits to be gracious, that He longs to pour out His blessing; that the love that gave the Son to death is the measure of the love that each moment hovers over every human being. **And yet He does not help."**

"And there they perish, a million a month in China alone, and it is as if God does not move. If He does so love and long to bless, there must be some inscrutable reason for His holding back. What can it be? **Scripture says, because of your unbelief.** It is the faithlessness and consequent unfaithfulness of God's people."

"He has taken them up into partnership with Himself; He has honoured them, and bound Himself, by making their prayers one of the standard measures of the working of His power. Lack of intercession is one of the chief causes of lack of blessing. Oh, that we would turn eye and heart from everything else and fix them upon this God who hears prayer, until the magnificence of His promises, and His power, and His purpose of love overwhelmed us! **How our whole life and heart would become intercession."**

Consider this: if God just calculated all of our needs but never bent to meet them – we would say that He had no mercy. However the world often views Him in just that light:

as angry, brooding, ever watching, always unwilling to help but ever ready to punish! However, no matter how wrong this picture is - do we fit that bill as well? In other words, do we just watch, judge and calculate other's needs, without ever acting in mercy or utilising prayer? With all the power available to us, do we not administer mercy and justice, as we should? *(Proverbs 31:8-9; Exodus 23:6)*

Lack of Prayer causes Lack of Blessing

Andrew Murray said above that, **"...lack of intercession is one of the chief causes of lack of blessing,"** and we know this to be true because James 4:2 put it in a nutshell by saying that **"we don't have because we don't ask!"** God has all the power and the resources of heaven and earth at His disposal, in order to answer our prayers, but who is praying?

His willingness and power without our cooperation on this earth - avails nothing! This fact that God has **"bound Himself, by making our prayers one of the standard measures of the working of His power"** makes each one of us tremendously accountable – we can hardly stand it! *(But again the Holy Spirit is our Helper!)*

Waiting for our Prayers

In addition to this, we know that throughout church history, revivals only occurred once a prayer campaign was well underway! In 2 Chronicles 7:14 we see confirmation of this... **"However, if my people, who are called by my name, will humble themselves, pray, search for me, and turn from their evil ways, then I will hear their prayer from heaven, forgive their sins, and heal their country"** *(GW).*

Our prayers are not made up of vain babblings, human reasonings and logical ideas. Yes our intellect is involved to a degree *(but even a child can pray)*, so it is not rocket science! Our prayers are based on faith, faith in God's Word alone. This is what pleases God and gets His attention - ABOVE ALL ELSE! *(Hebrews 11:6)*

Divine Conduits

With our prayers acting like a divine conduit or release-valve for all of heavens richest blessings it's imperative on us to make sure that God's abilities and willingness is never "held-back!"

Indeed God is waiting. Waiting for us! I agree with Andrew Murray; **how God's heart must *ache* for intercessors to rouse themselves.**

Let us be the ones!

❖

CHAPTER 4

Engage for Change

Intercession is an outstanding theme to focus on and all of us must be convicted to engage in this joint and wondrous responsibility.

We are all called to this servant's ministry, which really expresses the divine nature of God *(John 15:13)*. Intercession is an act of love – it takes obedience to pray. Most of us will agree that rarely have we ever *felt* like praying! It's not a feeling-orientated effort, although feelings do get involved. However love is an act of obedience first, then feelings follow. Such love *covers a multitude of sins,* even in our own lives! **In other words we directly benefit from the intercession that we do for others!** *(1 Peter 4:8)*

The Same Measure

Our attitude towards others really influences how God is obligated to handle us. For instance, although it's God's nature to forgive, we tie His hands every time we choose not to forgive. His Word says that if we don't forgive others then He can't forgive us *(Matthew 6:15; 18:22).*

This greatly impacts our salvation. People forget this and take God's promise of forgiveness for granted. People assume that they are heaven bound but what if this simple tenet escapes them? What if God refuses to recognise them, based solely on their treatment of others; their lack of forgiveness and love? **Then all other efforts will be undone** *(Matthew 7:23).*

Love before Obligation

Intercession is born out of love, before obligation. And it simply means: *one who took the place of, standing in the gap.* To intercede is to take the place of another, to stand in the gap on their behalf. Jesus' greatest act of intercession was to stand in the gap on the cross *(Isaiah 53:5-6).* However it is also our duty to stand in the gap for others in intercession.

"I look attentively, and there is none helping, And I am astonished that there is none supporting, and **give salvation to me doth mine own arm.** And my wrath - it hath supported me" *(Isaiah 63:5 YLT).* "He seeth that there is no man, And is **astonished that there is no intercessor,** And His own arm giveth salvation to Him, And His righteousness - it sustained Him" *(Isaiah 59:16 YLT).*

God is looking for intercessors simply because the Church has not taken its priestly place. "The people of the land practice extortion and commit robbery; they oppress the poor and needy and mistreat the foreigner, denying them justice. I looked for someone among them who would build up the wall and stand before me in the gap on behalf of the land so I would not have to destroy it, but I found no one. So I will pour out my wrath on them and consume them with my fiery anger, bringing down on their own heads all they have done, declares the Sovereign LORD" *(Ezekiel 22:29-31).*

Hedge of Protection

The scripture above just proves how people are bound to their own destruction; the wrath of God is already upon them BUT God wants us to take up our priestly ministry and stand in the gap for them. **Standing in the gap - literally means standing between these people and their destruction.** It's our priestly duty to make up the hedge and to protect them *(John 10:10).*

Looking at different translations can often give a sharper light to a subject. Take the book of Job for instance, chapter 9:32-33 from the New Living Translation where it says, "God is not a mortal like me, so I cannot argue with him or take him to trial. **If only there were a mediator between us, someone who could bring us together."**

Then in the same verse, perhaps with a slightly better edge on it, the Message Bible says, "God and I are not equals; I can't bring a case against him. We'll never enter a courtroom as peers. **How I wish we had an arbitrator to step in and let me get on with life...** Then I'd speak up and state my case boldly. As things stand, there is no way I can do it" *(Job 9:32-35 MSG).*

However as mediators or intercessors it is with the very Word of God that we defend people, pleading their case before God – according to His own Words. Mediators or intercessors are able to bring the very hand of God and the hand of man **together,** just as the New Living Translation nicely brought out above.

As a minister of the gospel, for more than a quarter of a century now, I still only see fruit during ministry, if the prayers of the saints have been offered up before hand. Only then can the rich fruit of ministry be reaped. It is the Church's duty to stand in the gap for people.

In the secular world however, someone who stands in the gap like this, in a legal manner is called an attorney. The Concise Oxford Dictionary gives the following definition for an attorney: **"one appointed to act for another** in business or legal matters *(who has power of attorney and authority to act thus)*, qualified lawyer, esp. representing clients in proceedings."

In this context, as intercessors, we too have been given power of attorney along with the authority to act on behalf of others; the only difference being that the law with which we specialise, is the perfect law of liberty in Christ!

Standing in their Place

This literally means to pray as if they were praying for themselves, so it is imperative that we pray the will of God not our own or even theirs. To do anything other than this would be to step into witchcraft.

Mostly this occurs unknowingly. None of us purposefully step into error. We tend not to realise that we are stepping over the boundaries and are convinced we're actually praying the will of God.

This is why we need the Holy Spirit so badly. He can rightly divide the Word in our hearts, so that out of our mouths flows revelation. We pray this revelation *(revealed truth)* into a situation, which helps us to hit target and not aimlessly beat the air!

The saying "practice makes perfect" suggests that if we do anything enough times, we become better at it. That's logic! As E.M Bounds would emphasize in his teaching *that* much time spent in the presence of God allows us to become better acquainted with His ways, more than someone who just makes pop-calls!

It is the Holy Spirit who reveals mysteries and gives revelation. We grow and mature. For example, what was a mystery to us just a year ago is no longer a mystery today. Because it's been revealed to us, as we spent time with Him. This means that the Holy Spirit is always increasing us on the inside. He does not keep us in a place of ignorance, so that we remain heavily dependent. No! He teaches us so that we can learn, grow and mature.

Prayer is an Active Event

Rend your heart, and not your garments, and turn unto the LORD your God: for he is gracious and merciful, slow to anger, and of great kindness.

(Joel 2:13 KJV)

To recap the principle meanings of intercession were:

- One who *took the place of*
- Standing in the gap

Then we looked at intercession in terms of providing a **hedge of protection** for others. Standing between them and the enemy, making up the hedge as mediators, defending them, by using the Word of God. We discussed the *power of attorney*, just like a lawyer who has the authority *to act on behalf of others* in a court of law.

Now we look at prayer as an *active event*. In the book of Isaiah 66:8 it says: "Who hath heard such a thing? Who hath seen such things? Shall the earth be made to bring forth in one day? Or shall a nation be born at once? For as soon as Zion *travailed,* she brought forth her children" *(KJV)*.

Instead of the word *travail* the NIV uses the word *labour*. Nevertheless this is a very profound statement, taking Zion *(as a type)* to represent the Church, the Body of Christ.

Spiritual Birthing

Stepping into *labour* or *travail* during intercession, is likened unto a state of *childbearing*. This type of praying then becomes a very active event, just like giving birth! Active in the contexts that intercession can sometimes require some strenuous *effort* and is not typically a passive enterprise! Just think, giving birth can be hard work and noisy. Not necessarily a pretty or pleasant experience either, in fact most mothers at that point, care very little who hears them scream!

So from this we can deduce that *travailing* in the spirit or *birthing* the things of God in prayer – can also be a noisy affair!

To add to this, I quote here from one of Jack Hayford's books on the subject, "Just as groans of travail precede birth, so Holy-Spirit-begotten intercessions forecast new life, new hope and new possibilities for individuals trapped in the impossible" (Hayford 144).

We can see in the book of Joel that God promises that if we rend our hearts, crying out and giving birth, that afterwards He will, "pour out His Spirit on all people" *(Joel 2:28)*.

A pouring forth of God's Spirit brings about "newness of life." However, there is more to the Spirit than just making us feel good! There is real passion that exists with the Spirit of God, to help individuals, to protect them, to intercede on their behalf and to be their advocate. Yet He still needs our prayers, to help Him bring this about. He needs us to work with Him in this passion of His, for people.

According to His Perfect Will

Let's consider at this point that God the Father is seen in a similar way as a judge, but is a judge who does not judge according to emotion or need, but according to TRUTH. As for us, we can pray no other way, except His perfect will.

"This is the confidence that we have in him, that, if we ask any thing **according to his will,** he heareth us" *(1 John 5:14 KJV)*. "In whom also we have obtained an inheritance, being predestinated according to the purpose of him who worketh all things **after the counsel of his own will**" *(Ephesians 1:11*

KJV). "He that searcheth the hearts knoweth what is the mind of the Spirit, because he maketh intercession for the saints **according to *the will* of God"** *(Romans 8:27 KJV).*

Scripture reveals to us that Satan has three main objectives: to steal, kill and to destroy *(John 10:10).* However God's not willing to just let that happen. He wants to intervene but needs our cooperation, to work closely with His Holy Spirit, so that destruction can be averted.

Stained by His Blood

Our Pass-Over-Lamb doesn't just want to *pass-over,* He wants to make a grand *entrance* and get involved. For example, in the Old Testament they just had their wooden doorframes and lintels stained with the animal's blood; Jesus however wants to cleanse, stain *(cover and protect)* our whole lives with His blood! This speaks of better things than the blood of Able and represents a covenant of much *better* things *(Hebrews 12:24).*

Let me add just swiftly that if the fathers of Israel had not followed God's divine instructions during those days in Egypt, they would have seen a much different outcome. The same is true of today. If we follow God's initiative, only then can we reap the desired results. God's *ways* work for those who *work* them and we have nothing to fear so long as we act *(including pray)* **according to His will.**

Vain and Delusive are Prayers without God's Sprit

Consider the fact that if praying were easy then we would not need a helper would we? However the Holy Spirit is our helper in prayer and as E.M Bounds wrote in his book, The

Reality of Prayer, **"How vain and delusive and how utterly fruitless and inefficient are prayers without the Sprit."** He goes on to say, **"...official prayers they may be, fitted for state occasion, beautiful and courtly, but worth less than nothing as God values prayer."**

However prayer is made easy through the ministry of the Holy Spirit working through us, but without His help, it's not difficult to suggest that we are useless at it! Yet travailing in the spirit does indeed bring forth new life, as we saw at the entrance of the tomb of Lazarus:

*When Jesus therefore saw her weeping, and the Jews also weeping which came with her, **he groaned in the spirit, and was troubled,** and said, Where have ye laid him? They said unto him, Lord, come and see. **Jesus wept.** Then said the Jews, Behold how he loved him! And some of them said, Could not this man, which opened the eyes of the blind, have caused that even this man should not have died?*

***Jesus therefore again groaning in himself cometh to the grave.** It was a cave, and a stone lay upon it. Jesus said, Take ye away the stone. Martha, the sister of him that was dead, saith unto him, Lord, by this time he stinketh: for he hath been dead four days.*

Jesus saith unto her, Said I not unto thee, that, if thou wouldest believe, thou shouldest see the glory of God? Then they took away the stone from the place where the dead was laid. And Jesus lifted up his eyes, and said, Father, I thank thee that thou hast heard me. And I knew that thou hearest me always: but because of the people which stand by I said it, that they may believe that thou hast sent me.

And when he thus had spoken, **he cried with a loud voice, Lazarus, come forth.** *And he that was dead came forth, bound hand and foot with graveclothes: and his face was bound about with a napkin. Jesus saith unto them,* **Loose him, and let him go.**

(John 11:33-44 KJV)

Out Loud

Now there is so much in these verses above that we could dissect them all day long! Yet just by highlighting certain parts of it in bold font – it's easy to see that Jesus was not quiet during this event. It was not a moment where Jesus was looking to be *discreet* rather it was an event where everyone heard!

According to the King James Version, it says expressly that Jesus **"groaned," "wept" and "cried with a loud voice."** Jesus was NOT hidden away somewhere in a private prayer closet, but was **openly travailing in the Spirit.**

By way of small interjection here – **if Jesus needed the Holy Spirit in prayer, how much more do we?**

Jesus used the Opportunity

Moving on, I draw your attention to notice how the people said, "...behold how he loved him!" because they saw Him cry, "Jesus wept." People very often only know how to read emotions, however emotions rarely give an accurate reading! Those present that day did likewise; they put everything down to *emotion* and *sentiment* rather than accurately reading what was truly taking place.

For instance, if Jesus was just all bent-out-of-shape emotionally, as they supposed *(because a good friend had died)*, then why did He purposefully delay His arrival two full days? "Therefore his sisters sent unto him, saying, Lord, behold, he whom thou lovest is sick. When Jesus heard that, he said, this sickness is not unto death, but for the glory of God, that the Son of God might be glorified thereby.

Now Jesus loved Martha, and her sister, and Lazarus. When he had heard therefore that he was sick, **he abode two days still in the same place where he was.** Then after that saith he to *his* disciples, Let us go into Judea again" *(John 11:3-7 KJV)*.

The truth of the matter is that there was a purpose to this event, which Jesus was savvy to. It was *not* an emotion that Jesus was yielding to but an opportunity to reveal how God answers prayer.

Travail Released New Life

Travail brings life. It did then and still can today. This type of prayer is so active because *new life* is involved. Just as a new baby must be pushed out into the world, so must new life, new hope, new vision etc. The miracles of God must be pushed into existence. His will must be done on earth as it already manifests in heaven, being released into this earth's realm through intercession and travail.

A good example of this vital process is where Daniel prayed with perseverance and the angel who carried God's answer was delayed in arriving: "Then said he unto me, Fear not, Daniel: for **from the *first* day** that thou didst set thine heart to understand, and to chasten thyself before thy God, **thy words were heard, and I am come for thy words**" *(Daniel 10:12 KJV).*

It goes on to say, "But the prince of the kingdom of Persia **withstood me one and twenty days:** but, lo, Michael, one of the chief princes, came to help me; and I remained there with the kings of Persia."

Spiritual Warfare

This was spiritual warfare being spoken of here. Notice how Daniel did not quit praying until the breakthrough came. This takes perseverance – something that we must adopt in our praying. It takes courage to wait without growing faint.

In fact it will do us good to remember what the angel told Daniel, that how on the very *first* day that he prayed, the answer was released from heaven and was making its journey to earth! But it took all of 21 days to get there. Do we quit before it arrives? Do we realise that our prayers are as good as answered the first day we pray, but the manifestation of those answers takes a little longer to materialise?

Victory and Forgotten Pain

Going back to travail, when a woman is giving birth, as Jesus foretold, it is agony. But a moment after the child is born and laid upon the mother's breast, the pain is forgotten and the joy of the new birth overwhelms her. We can remember this, because there is a lot of joy connected with intercession. An intense joy that comes with the breakthrough and the victory!

When interceding, there will be times when we know in the spirit that the breakthrough happened. We will know this breakthrough by the experience of JOY! Now this speaks of more than just emotion, but of reality. There is a difference! We must decide to rejoice that our prayers have been received and answered in the spirit realm, perhaps long before we see any results in the natural realm. **Prayer is all about faith. Praying faith,** speaking those things that are not as thought they were! *(Romans 4:17)*

Intercession is a very powerful weapon in spiritual warfare, it is indeed a powerful weapon in the onslaught against the enemy; Satan does not like it. If you want to see the Spirit of God move more than He has already, whether in the local church, school, and housing estate or even in a specific relationship that involves people who are not born again, then we MUST be willing to intercede. We must be of an attitude that allows the will of God to be **brought into being,** and travail for those in need. Then we will reap the harvest, which God has prepared.

Paul in Galatians 4:19 said, "My dear children, for whom I am again in the pains of childbirth until Christ is formed in you." **Paul was constantly in a place of weeping before God for his people.**

This then must also be the place for us.

Third Pillar

RIGHTEOUSNESS

❖

CHAPTER 5

The Reality of Righteousness

We now come to our third pillar, righteousness. In Romans chapter 3, beginning with verse 20 *(KJV)* it says, "Therefore by the deeds of the law there shall no flesh be justified *(lit. **declared** righteous)*, in his sight; for by the law is the knowledge of sin."

"But now God has shown us a way to be made right with him without keeping the requirements of the law, as was promised in the writings of Moses and the prophets long ago.

We are made right with God by repenting of our sin and placing our faith in Jesus Christ. And this is true for everyone who believes, no matter who we are."

*For everyone has sinned... Yet God, with undeserved kindness, **declares** that we are righteous.*

(Romans 3:23-24 NLT)

Perfect Atonement

Dr. Michael Brown in Charisma News writes about a e-devotional titled "ONLY CHRIST'S ATONEMENT SATISFIES GOD" by Pastor Prince. He says that Prince rightly points us to the shed blood of the Messiah for our atonement, stating, "Because of His sacrifice, all our sins have already been perfectly atoned for. That is why, should we sin, we know that 'we have an Advocate with the Father, Jesus Christ the righteous.' And He Himself is the propitiation for our sins."

Pastor Prince also emphasized that it is not our acts of self-mortification that bring us forgiveness — not whipping ourselves or beating ourselves or fasting for days or praying for hours — but rather what Jesus did on our behalf.

He writes, "My friend, there is no need to climb the Himalayas or whip your back bloody to atone for your sins. No amount of self-punishment or crying can atone for them. Your sins have already been punished fully in the body of Jesus. Only His finished work satisfies God."

This is a life-giving, life-transforming message, and it is one that can deliver us from a legalistic, work-righteousness, earn-your-salvation mentality that plagues many believers.

We are saved by Jesus' righteousness, not our own righteousness! May we never forget that as long as we live.

Unfortunately, as is common with the <u>hyper-grace message</u>, there is a mixture of beautiful truth with potentially dangerous error.

Citing 1 John 2:1-2, Pastor Prince writes, "Now, it does not say that if anyone repents, we have an Advocate with the Father. It says that if anyone sins, we have an Advocate with the Father. The moment a child of God sins, straightaway, his Advocate, Jesus Christ, goes into action to pray for and protect him."

Sin without Consequence

Does that mean, then, that I can continue in sin without consequence? Does that mean that, the more I rebel and the more I turn away from God, the more Jesus forgives me?

You might say, "But that's not the point Pastor Prince was making. He's teaching believers not to get caught up in fleshly efforts of 'repentance' and rather to find forgiveness in the cross."

Of course, I understand that, and I applaud that. Shout that from the rooftops, Pastor Prince. I know you already do.

But since he never once says in the article that it's important that we turn from sin to be in right relationship with God *(something taught throughout the entire New Testament)*, and since he wrongly defines repentance *(more on that in a moment)*, how is someone to know that it's important that we do not continue in sin?

Perhaps Pastor Prince could have added in even one line to the effect?

After all, why quote 1 John 2:1-2 without also quoting the next two verses? John continued, "By this we know that we know Him, if we keep His commandments. Whoever says, 'I know Him,' and does not keep His commandments is a liar, and the truth is not in him" *(1 John 2:3-4)*. Would this undermine one of Pastor Prince's points?

And how about some of these other verses from 1 John? Would the reader of Pastor Prince's e-devotional realize that this also was John's message?

- "If we say that we have fellowship with Him, yet walk in darkness, we lie and do not practice the truth" *(1 John 1:6)*

- "Whoever says he is in the light but hates his brother is in darkness even until now" *(1 John 2:9)*

- "Whoever practices sin breaks the law, for sin is lawlessness. You know that He was revealed to take away our sins, and in Him there is no sin. Whoever remains in Him does not sin. Whoever sins has not seen Him and does not know Him" *(1 John 3:4-6)*

- "Whoever practices sin is of the devil, for the devil has been sinning from the beginning. For this purpose the Son of God was revealed, that He might destroy the works of the devil. Whoever has been born of God does not practice sin, for His seed remains in him. And he cannot keep on sinning, because he has been born of God" *(1 John 3:8-9)*

- "Now the one who keeps His commandments remains in Him, and He in him" *(1 John 3:24)*

- "By this we know that we love the children of God: when we love God and keep His commandments. For this is the love of God, that we keep His commandments. And His commandments are not burdensome" *(1 John 5:2-3)*

Yes, it is absolutely true that Jesus paid for our sins and our atonement is found in Him alone. And it is equally true that He saves us out of sin, calls us out of sin and, as our Lord and King, commands us and empowers us to turn from sin.

That is also an essential part of the gospel message, and in a devotional that misrepresents repentance and states that, "The moment a child of God sins, straightaway, his Advocate, Jesus Christ, goes into action to pray for and protect him," this is a potentially fatal omission.

Repentance a change of Mind?

With regard, then, to repentance, Pastor Prince rightly states that, "Bible repentance is not this idea of hitting or punishing yourself to atone for your sins." But he wrongly states that, "The word 'repentance' is *metanoia* in the Greek, which means to change one's mind." Not so, although this is a very common error.

"Repentance" in the bible means a change of mind, heart and direction. It means the recognition that you are heading the wrong way on the highway, then making a complete about face - with God's help and grace - and heading in a brand-new direction. But if you recognize you're heading in the wrong direction - in other words, you have a change of mind - but you don't turn around, you have not repented in the biblical sense of the word.

And how important is repentance for the believer?

According to Jesus, it's very important.

That's why, five separate times, he told congregations in Asia Minor *(to paraphrase)*, "If you want to be in right relationship with Me, repent and change your ways" *(see Revelation 2:5, 16, 21-22; 3:3, 19)*.

To quote the Lord's own words, "Those whom I love, I rebuke and discipline. Therefore be zealous and repent. Listen! I stand at the door and knock. If anyone hears My voice and opens the door, I will come in and dine with him, and he with Me" *(Revelation 3:19-20)*.

And so as we celebrate the atonement we enjoy in Jesus the Messiah, let us always remember that He sets us free from sin, not to sin, and that forgiveness and repentance go hand in hand.

Looking to the Cross

So we look to the cross, where our sins were paid for in full, and, empowered by the Spirit of God, we confess our sins *(see 1 John 1:9, which is primarily written to believers, not the lost)*, we renounce those sins, and being washed and cleansed by His blood, we turn away from those sins.

As expressed so powerfully by Peter, "He Himself bore our sins in His own body on the tree, that we, being dead to sins, should live unto righteousness. 'By His wounds you were healed.' For you were as sheep going astray, but now have been returned to the Shepherd and Guardian of your souls" *(1 Peter 2:24-25)*.

That is the message of atonement.

Dr. Michael Brown *(www.askdrbrown.org)* is the host of the nationally syndicated Line of Fire radio program. His latest book is The Grace Controversy.

God's Declaration over Us

"For everyone has sinned; we all fall short of God's glorious standard. Yet God, with undeserved kindness, **declares that we are righteous.** He did this through Christ Jesus when He freed us from the penalty for our sins. For God presented Jesus as the sacrifice for sin. People are made right with God when they believe that Jesus sacrificed his life, shedding his blood.

This sacrifice shows that God was being fair when he held back and did not punish those who sinned in times past for he was looking ahead and including them in what he would do in this present time. God did this to demonstrate his righteousness, for he himself is fair and just, and he declares sinners to be right in his sight when they believe in Jesus" *(Romans 3:21-26 NLT).*

In the King James Version, verse 26 it reads like this: "To declare, I say, at this time his righteousness: that he might be *just,* and the *justifier* of him which believeth in Jesus."

Affirmation of Innocence

The writers of the King James Version chose to use the words *just* and *justifier,* which means: *to render or declare innocent/righteous.* So from this passage we can see that righteousness is not attainable through our own efforts. It has to come from God and in His economy of things, there is nothing any of us can do to "render or declare" ourselves righteous. Thank God this is the case, because if good works were necessary, then ten million good works would never be enough!

The Deception of Self Righteousness

Deception always whispers, "You don't need God!" and those who believe this are amongst those who are still convinced of their own righteousness. What they don't realise is that it's Christ's righteousness they need not their own.

However this type of religious deception is a very subtle; the most well meaning folks still have it in the back of their minds that mere "church-attendance" weighs in somewhere in helping to make them righteous!

Others believe that good deeds, like selling chicken-dinners or holding fund-raisers in support of God's program help make them righteous! But no kind of fund-raiser will even come close to procuring even the smallest of heavenly *favours*, let alone any divine contributions towards being righteous! Not a single *good work* can do it!

The only solution offered us is Jesus. He is all we need! We are righteous because of Him and not independent of Him. We cannot look from afar *at* Him and think we can have what He has. The only way we can obtain righteousness, is to be IN Christ Jesus, because God counts the righteousness of Christ as valid, not ours, "...we are all as an unclean *thing, and all **our** righteousness's *are* as **filthy rags**..." (Isaiah 64:6 KJV)*

Consider it like this. In the Old Testament righteousness was gained through faith *(see Hebrews chapter 11 for the great hall of faith!)* Now in the New Testament it is no longer so. We can only gain righteousness by receiving the One who *is* righteousness!

Holiness owns an Innocent Lifestyle

Our *own* is filthy as said in the scripture above and this is where holiness comes into it. **Holiness is part of righteousness,** because righteousness also means *innocence.* **Holiness is an innocent lifestyle;** however the only innocent one among us is Christ; blameless and pure. "Be holy because I, the LORD, am holy. I set you apart as holy" *(Leviticus 21:8 GW).*

We are encouraged over and over again throughout scripture to stay far away from any kind of perversion, which is the exact opposite of holiness. Perversion is that which can stain our white *(blood washed)* robes of righteousness.

We must *remain* spiritually clean once Christ has cleansed us because, "Christ also loved the church, and gave himself for it; That he might sanctify and **cleanse** it with the washing of water by the word, That he might present it to himself a glorious church, **not having spot, or wrinkle,** or any such thing; but that it should be **holy and without blemish**" *(Ephesians 5:25-27 KJV).*

Only the Holy Spirit can help do the impossible, "remain spotless, pure and blameless," in a dark world full of filth. After all God did give us His Spirit of holiness.

Clean Slate

Therefore it stands to reason that once God has *declared* us righteous in His sight, through Christ, we have a clean slate and an innocent record. We cannot corrupt this again by continuing in sin and expecting our innocent status to go unaffected. As those who tout: "once saved *always* saved," also fail to understand that it is possible to *disrobe*. In other words, we can take off our robes of righteousness anytime! We can also compromise them at any time. That's why we must continue in righteousness and work out our salvation with "fear and trembling" *(Philippians 2:12)*.

You can reject them *(robes)* and the blood that bought them anytime; but God's desire "that none should perish," will never alter. He can never change, as there is no "variableness, neither shadow of turning" with Him *(James 1:17 KJV)*.

Remaining Innocent

On the other hand *we* change all the time! Yet we must remain innocent. The only way to achieve this is to remain in Christ's innocence and righteousness. Only *in* Christ is this possible. From start to finish and all the way through... we must keep our eyes on Christ and stay in Him. Without Christ, we have no qualification. God the Father sees, even the demons in hell see this righteousness of Christ, in and on our lives *(they must recognise Christ - see "Seven sons of Sceva" Acts 19:14)*.

The righteousness of God revealed: "For I am not ashamed of the gospel of Christ: for it is the power of God unto salvation to everyone that believeth; to the Jew first, and also to the Greek. For therein is the righteousness *(dikaiosunē)* of God revealed from faith to faith: as it is written. The just shall live by faith. For the wrath of God is revealed from heaven against all ungodliness and unrighteousness *(adikia)* of men, who hold the truth in unrighteousness" *(Romans 1:16-18 KJV)*.

In the New Testament the Greek word for righteousness used above in Romans 1:16-18 is *dikaiosunē (pronounced dik-ah-yos-oo'-nay)*, Strong's #G1343, lit. equity *(of character or act)*; specifically *(Christian)* justification. Then the Greek word for **"unrighteousness"** also used above in Romans 1:16-18 is adikia *(pronounced ad-ee-kee'-ah)*, Strong's #G93, lit. *(legal)* injustice *(properly, the quality, by implication, the act)*; moral wrongfulness *(of character, life or act): -* iniquity, unjust, wrong.

In the Old Testament we see the Hebrew word used for righteousness in one of the names of God Jehovah-Tsidkenu -yehôvâhtsidqênû *(pronounced yeh-ho-vaw' tsid-kay'-noo)* Strong's #H3072 which describes this name as a symbolical epithet of the Messiah and of Jerusalem: - The Lord Our Righteousness.

Not Earned or Bought

Like grace, righteousness as a *gift* cannot be earned or bought; a gift is *given* and is the total prerogative of the giver not the receiver! When it comes to the gift of righteousness, we must be declared righteous by the giver - God. When

He declares us righteous, then we are righteous! Notice that righteousness was also called a *gift* in Romans 5:17 *(KJV)*, "...they which receive abundance of **grace** and of the **gift of righteousness** shall reign in life by one, Jesus Christ."

A gift is something that one person gives to another, and is given willingly. It can't be bought or worked for. If it could, it would cease to be a gift. It would become a wage or a payment. But when a gift is given, obligation free and voluntarily, then it is a total gift. There's nothing left to do but *receive* or *reject* it!

As righteousness is such a gift all we must do is receive it. In fact at the same moment we received Jesus Christ as our personal Lord and Saviour; right at that moment, God gave us the gift of righteousness.

"Therefore, as by the offence of one judgement came upon all men to condemnation; even so by the righteousness of one the free gift came upon all men unto justification of life" *(verse 18 KJV)*.

Many *will* be made Righteous

The word condemnation means judgement. By the righteousness of Jesus Christ, this free gift came upon all men unto justification or unto the declaration of righteousness. "For just as by one man's disobedience *(failing to hear, heedlessness, and carelessness)* the many were constituted sinners, so by one man's obedience the **many *will* be constituted righteous** *(made acceptable to God, brought into right standing with Him)*" *(verse 19 AMP)*.

Notice, how affirmative this is: "many *will* be made righteous." It did not say that, "many *might* be made righteousness if they work hard enough to earn it!" Just as righteousness is not something we earn neither is it something we replicate. It is purely something that God does for us. Because of Christ we are as righteous as we are ever going to get! In other words it's all because of Him. Start to finish. We can't initiate it or improve on it. IT IS DONE. When we stepped into Christ, we stepped into *His* righteousness. Pure and simple!

When I used to think that I had to *do* things to become righteous, I inevitably failed, *(no matter my efforts or good intentions)*, as a result I felt even more un-righteous! What I failed to comprehend was that God had already declared me righteous through Christ. God's Word is final authority on the subject; it's all about what He says, not what we say about ourselves, our feelings *(or even our denominations!)*

Reigning in *this* Life

It's easy to feel un-righteous at times, but that's precisely why it takes faith and not feelings to affirm the Word of God and declare, **"I am the righteousness of God in Christ Jesus!"** *(2 Corinthians 5:21)*

*For if because of one man's trespass (lapse, offense) death reigned through that one, much more surely will those who receive [God's] overflowing grace (unmerited favour) and the free gift of righteousness [putting them into right standing with Himself] **reign as kings in life** through the one Man Jesus Christ (the Messiah, the Anointed One).*
(Romans 5:17 AMP)

What an awesome concept - **reigning in this life!** To reign is terminology normally used for kings who rule their own kingdom and this is precisely what the word "reign" literally means, *to rule*. However let me point out, that we are not just meant to rule in the next life but right here in this one. **Reign in life right now, right here today!**

I prefer the Amplified Version of the above scripture, which says, *"Shall reign as kings in life."* In other words we are meant to rule our circumstances and everything in our immediate environment, to exert influence all around us, just as Jesus did.

Taking Dominion One-Step at a Time

From the Old Testament let's use Elijah and Elisha as our example. In 2 Kings 2:8-14 we see Elijah and Elisha *(first together, then Elisha alone)* wanted to cross the Jordan River and there were no bridges or ferries to take them across, so verse 8 says, "Elijah took his cloak, rolled it up and struck the water with it. The water divided to the right and to the left, and the two of them crossed over on dry ground."

Then verses 13-14 continues with Elisha as, "He picked up the cloak that had fallen from Elijah and went back and stood on the bank of the Jordan. Then he took the cloak that had fallen from him and struck the water with it. 'Where now is the LORD, the God of Elijah?' he asked. When he struck the water, it divided to the right and to the left, and he crossed over."

In closing, just imagine the scene here; he took his mantle from around his neck and slapped the water with it.

Everywhere he *slapped* the water, dry land appeared. As the water drew back, he stepped out onto that dry patch and then slapped the water again, until he eventually walked across on dry land. **Taking dominion one-step at a time!**

Now this is exactly how we should treat the circumstances of life. Take authority one *slap* at a time! When we truly walk with God, we reign with Him and even the elements cannot withstand our faith in Him. *(Remember Jesus is King of kings and Lord of lords. If we reign with Him this makes us kings and lords!)*

Finally: Elijah was such a one who dared to reign in this life with God and when he prayed it literally didn't rain for three-and-one-half years. He **ruled** the circumstances. Jesus stopped a storm by telling the sea to be still and the waves to lie down - they did!

Then He said,

> *I tell you for certain that if you have faith in me, you will do the same things that I am doing. You will do even greater things, now that I am going back to the Father.*
> *(John 14:12 CEV)*

As followers of Christ, we too are supposed to be the *masters* of our circumstances.

❖

CHAPTER 6

Masters of our Circumstances

I love to see people succeed in life, just like the artist treasures his painting and the craftsman his violin, so our Creator cherishes His design! He is concerned about our dreams, goals and our ability to be happy and to enjoy life. But all said and done, none of us can truly enjoy life unless we STAY IN OUR RIGHT MINDS!

For as he thinketh in his heart, so is he...
(Proverbs 23:7 KJV)

Success is being happy. Happiness is basically feeling good about our lives and plans. **Two forces are vital to happiness: our relationships and our achievements.**

The Gospel also has two forces, the Person of Jesus Christ, and the principles He taught:

- One is the Son of God; the other is the system of God

- One is the life of God; the other is the law of God

- One is the King; the other is the Kingdom

- One is an experience with God; the other is the expertise of God

- One is heart-related the other is mind-related

Salvation is experienced *"instantaneously"* while God's wisdom principles are learned *"progressively,"* and both are essential for success and happiness.

In everything therefore we must make it a priority to protect our thought lives. Some folks like to shout about their "double portion" but have never dealt with their fanatic in the attic *(the mind)!* In reality the same Holy Spirit will make us deal with this chief opponent *first;* there is no uncertainty about it, we must conquer our minds! This is a place where there can be no demilitarised zone, no middle ground. Either it belongs to the enemy or to God.

Discipline vs. Torment

When it comes to the mind there is no grey fudge. It is black or white, all or nothing. Another thing is for certain; **where there is no discipline there is no Holy Spirit!** He is never chaos. He is always order! Anyone who is successful today *(whether secular or Christian)* is someone who has mastered his or her mind with sheer "discipline." From businessmen to politicians, sports personnel or record breakers, they set their "minds" on a goal and don't deviate.

Sadly in retrospect many Christians are incapacitated *(out of action)* because they have never learnt how to protect their thought lives. Satan torments them with fear, hatred, suspicion, depression, mistrust and a host of other mental distractions *(or should I say disorders?)*

So why does this zone *(the mind)* have to be the most vulnerable area of our lives? Because happiness really does begin between our ears! **The mind is the drawing room for tomorrow's successes or failures;** what happens there, happens in time. As scripture clearly tells us *"...as he thinketh in his heart, so is he" (Proverbs 23:7 KJV).* So what you "keep in mind" from day to day is really what is shaping your future, whether positive or negative! Making "mind-management" a MUST for any believer who seeks to be an over-comer!

In fact it's not hard to recognise an over-comer from a defeatist, simply someone who is self-adjusting vs. someone who lives in perpetual internal chaos and confusion, and their outer world usually shows it too!

A Complete inward Renovation

Conquering or mastering the mind can be called *renewing* the mind, which is why Paul wrote to the Romans saying, "Do not conform any longer to the pattern of this world, but be transformed by the *renewing* of your mind. Then you will be able to test and approve what God's will is - his good, pleasing and perfect will" *(Romans 12:2).* Our minds must be renewed because God's salvation includes the mind.

The original Greek language for renewal *anakaínōsis (an-ak-ah'-ee-no-sis - see Strong's #G342)* refers to: a renewal or change of heart and life. To renovation, complete change for the better, a fresh and new development achieved by God's power.

The late Dr. Bob Gordon said, "The mind is an actual battlefield in the experience of many people. Lack of mental discipline leads to chaos in the thought life, an inability to discern truth from error and bondage to an imagination that is able to breed negative ideas and dreams."

In her bestseller, *"The Battlefield of the Mind"* Joyce Meyer also states that there is a war going on where our minds are the battlefield, the good news being that God is fighting on our side! In her book Joyce uncovers the tactics of the enemy and gives a clear-cut plan to triumph in the fight for your mind. She teaches how to renew the mind through the Word and stand victoriously in the battlefield of the mind.

Overcoming a Corrosive Thought Life

Our enemy uses a deliberately devised plan of deceit and lies, attacking our minds with doubting thoughts, fear and paranoia to erode our resistance, investing any amount of time in order to defeat us.

However the Word of God has the power to cleanse our minds regardless and it is all-important that we read and meditate on His Word, remaining obedient to it. We must read, meditate and speak the Word continually, **taking captive every thought to make it obedient to Christ** *(2 Corinthians 10:5).*

The following scriptures reveal the weaknesses of our natural mind:

- It is hostile to God *(Romans 8:5-7)*, unbelievers are often *hostile* towards the gospel

- The things of God are foolish to the natural mind *(1 Corinthians 2:12-14)*

- Satan blinds the natural mind from seeing God *(2 Corinthians 4:4)*

- The natural mind is the source of violent and evil desires *(Ephesians 2:3)* depraved *(Romans 1:28)*

- The natural mind is futile in its thinking and darkened in its understanding *(Ephesians 4:17-18)*

Do not let this book of the law depart from your mouth; **meditate on it day and night,** *so that you may be careful to do everything written in it. Then you will be prosperous and successful.*

(Joshua 1:8)

Obeying Natural Instincts vs. God

Perhaps you can imagine how Joshua might have felt after he had just successfully crossed over the Jordan River through an awesome act of faith; which took him and all the people across only to arrive at Jericho to look up and see those gigantic walls that surrounded that great city.

As a military man his mind must have gone to work strategizing, "Well if we build some ramps, we'll come at it like this... we can make a hole and maybe get through..." But instead of *attacking* those walls, God's instructions were to *march* around them in silence for seven long and probably hot days - surely this sounded so foolish to Joshua's naturally military mind?

Joshua was as natural as you or I; it would have been as much of a discipline for him as for us - to be disciplined enough to flow with the mind of God not his own instincts. Especially when the instructions were so *un-natural* and out of sync with his natural instincts! So as a military figure Joshua had to lay down his own strategies and agendas in order to accept the Lord's.

A Determined and Deliberate Act of Faith

This is not always easy. But then submission rarely is! It's based on trust, faith and relationship and dying to self! But as we know on the seventh day when they all marched around in obedience seven times *shouting and praising* the Lord, it was then and only then - out of sheer obedience and discipline - that the walls came tumbling down. **Let's be honest, it takes a disciplined mind just to keep our mouths quiet!** "For out of the abundance *(overflow)* of the heart, his mouth speaks!" *(Luke 6:45 AMP)*

Remember this - faith is not chatty or spontaneous - it is too deliberate! **Disciplining our minds has to be a determined and deliberate act of faith.** Only then can we say that we have conquered and renewed our minds, and have "the mind of Christ" *(1 Corinthians 2:16)*.

Signs of a Renewed Mind

Casting down imaginations, and every high thing that exalteth itself against the knowledge of God, and bringing into captivity every thought to the obedience of Christ...
(2 Corinthians 10:4-5 KJV)

I want to give you some examples from scripture of what a renewed *(renovated or reconditioned)* mind looks like!

- Our spiritual understanding is increased *(Ephesians 1:18)*

- Our minds become the vehicle of the Holy Spirit and His gifts, discernment and revelation

- We have a changed life through understanding truth, where we take the cleansing power of God's Word to sanctify our minds and set us free from wrong thoughts

Paul in Ephesians told us to put off the old self, which is being corrupted by its deceitful desires. To be made new in the attitude of our minds; and to put on the *new* self, created to be like God in true righteousness and holiness *(see Ephesians 4:22-24; Hebrews 4:12).*

- We have surrendered our minds completely as well as our bodies to the Lord *(Romans 12:1)*

Relying totally on the Holy Spirit

I remember a healing evangelist Ian Andrews from Chard, Somerset UK once say, that when he began to minister in the early 70's, he was told to *"go and preach the gospel"* but by the time he had stuttered the words *"g o od - m o r n i n g"* it was already *afternoon!* Ian prayed *"Lord heal me of my stutter and 'then' I will go and preach the gospel for You."*

Nonetheless people were still going to Ian with all kinds of stuttering problems and were getting healed *left-right-*

and-centre, which made it even more frustrating for him. However through that process **God taught Ian Andrews how to rely totally on the Holy Spirit** and not upon his own understanding, strengths or circumstances, a good lesson for all of us!

Ian had suffered with a severe stammer for most of his life and would say to God, *"Lord I'd be thrilled to preach the gospel and pray for the sick - only heal me first."*

Obedience brings Breakthrough

Except God had the last word on the subject, *"No! You go as you are, then everyone will know who the Healer is - that it's Me. Go and I will heal you... AS YOU GO."* And that is precisely what happened! As Ian moved in obedience, God healed him gradually.

For Ian, it was a humbling and sometimes frustrating experience and yet he found that yielding to God was the only way forward. And to his surprise, God's life began to flow through him. People were getting healed. But most importantly nothing depended on Ian or how he *felt.*

Simply as Ian kept pointing people to Jesus and telling them that Jesus had taken their pains and sicknesses upon Himself, they just looked to God and were healed, pure and simple!

Ian Andrews is the Apostolic Director of the International Association of Healing Ministries *(www.iequippers.org)* and the Founder of Citadel Ministries *(www.citadelministries.com).* He has been actively a leading figure in the healing ministry for more than four decades and has authored the following two books: Equipped to Heal *(Onwards and Upwards Publications, UK, 2011)*; Healed by His Stripes *(TEC Publications, USA)*.

The Holy Spirit and the Renewal Process

Our greatest need right now as Christians is the Holy Spirit. He is the only one who can help us understand the profoundness of all of these things. He alone can show us just how to go about renewing our minds.

These few steps are part of the process:

- First we must *completely* surrender our minds to the Lord *(Romans 12:1)*. Complete means complete! This is not a weight watchers plan that we join for a few weeks till normal life resumes again. NO! This is God we are talking about and what He does in our lives is for *keeps*. The idea is this, we give Him our minds and He gives us the Mind of Christ. *It's more than a fair deal I would say! In fact it is a pure act of grace*

- Then we must submit *all* of our thinking to the cross *(2 Corinthians 10:5)*

- We must make continual and deliberate choices where to place of our minds *(Colossians 3:2)*

- We must always read and meditate on the cleansing power of God's Word *(Joshua 1:8)*

- We must examine and test the content of our thought lives. Whatever comes in we must test: is this of God or not? Is it of the flesh or of the Spirit? *(Philippians 4:8-9)*

- We must *immediately* filter and refuse every thought that is wrong or sinful *(and not flirt with them!)* God's Word says that we should think of things that are pure, honest and true. The devil wants the opposite kind of thinking going on in our heads! He knows just how destructive our thought lives can be

- We must commit to thinking God's thoughts

- We do this by reading and meditating on His Word: "Do not let this book of the law depart from your mouth; meditate on it day and night, so that you may be careful to do everything written in it. Then you will be prosperous and successful" *(Joshua 1:8)*

Jesus Resisted Human Reasoning

When a situation comes up, we must *not* deal with it by human reasoning. Why? Remember that Jesus explained to His disciples that He must go to Jerusalem and suffer many things, even unto death, but Peter rebuked Him saying, "Never, Lord! This shall never happen to you!"

And Jesus turned to him and said, "Get behind Me, Satan! You are a stumbling block to me; you do not have in mind the things of God, but the things of men" *(Matthew 16:21-23)*.

Consider this... just momentarily. Linger on what Jesus said, **"...you have not in mind the things of God but the things of men."** Often what we have in mind is *absolutely everything!* But the serious Christian must mind the things of God and not the things of this world.

It is not enough to think about something that needs our decision or prayer. We must think about it the way God thinks about it.

For example God's thoughts went beyond the suffering that Jesus would encounter in Jerusalem, beyond the rejection, humiliation, the cross and the grave. In fact God's thoughts looked forward to the resurrection, the triumphant ascension, the outpouring of the Holy Spirit, to Christ's glorious second coming, and ultimately towards His eternal sovereign reign upon this earth.

Change daily Priorities

Dr. Mike Murdock says the following: We must secure all pertinent information concerning our goals. "Wise men lay up knowledge..." *(Proverbs 10:14 KJV)* "My people are destroyed for lack of knowledge..." *(Hosea 4:6 KJV)* Observe. Read. Maintain an "information file." Utilise the expertise of others. "He that walketh with wise men shall be wise..." *(Proverbs 13:20 KJV)*

Create a climate of confidence in every circumstance:

We must speak about our expectations of success, not our experiences or failures. "Death and life are in the power of the tongue..." *(Proverbs 18:21 KJV)* We must rehearse previous achievements in our minds and remember that our sufficiency is of God. "In whom we have boldness and access with confidence by the faith of him" *(2 Corinthians 3:5; Ephesians 3:11)*. **Our position of superiority over circumstances was established when we became children of God** *(Romans 8:16, 17, 37)*.

Help others become successful:

Assist others in discovering their gifts, talents and dreams. You will reap what you sow. The motto of the way of the winner is, **"What you make happen for others, God will make happen to you."** When Job prayed for his friends, his captivity was turned *(Job 42:10)*. When the poor widow gave to the prophet, God gave to her *(1 Kings 17)*. "Knowing that whatsoever good thing any man doeth, the same shall he receive of the Lord" *(Ephesians 6:8 KJV)*.

Value the God connection:

Recognise God as a plus factor. He is never a disadvantage to us, always an asset. He wants us to succeed and He "hath pleasure in the prosperity of His servant" *(Psalm 35:27 KJV)*. Read scriptures on a daily schedule. Practise the power of prayer. Make Jesus Christ Lord of your life. "Acquaint now thyself with him, and be at peace: thereby good shall come unto thee" *(Job 22:21 KJV)*; "...as long as he sought the Lord, God made him to prosper" *(2 Chronicles 26:5 KJV)*.

Our thinking must be disciplined. Only then can we have success. "Life only changes when our daily priorities change."

Mike Murdock goes on to say, "Winners are simply ex-losers who got mad. Winning doesn't start *around* you it begins *inside* you. So make up your mind!"

What happens in your mind will happen in time.

Fourth Pillar

OBEDIENCE

❖

CHAPTER 7

Fearless Willingness

So many people write to me asking about how to get a closer relationship with the Holy Spirit. Wanting to know how to hear, sense, feel or receive the Holy Spirit. So I want to quote verbatim one of my readers, who simply asked:

"I have really been desiring a closer fellowship with the Holy Spirit, but don't seem to have gotten heaven's attention yet. Possibly because I don't mediate enough or pray enough. I have been born again but still don't feel the fellowship of the Holy Spirit. What can I be doing wrong or not doing? I don't seem to have any gift of the Spirit except speaking in other tongues. Can you tell me what to do and pray along with me?"

My initial response was, "Stop trying too hard!" Because it has always pained me to see sincere people *half-*

killing-themselves to get more of God and then missing Him completely!

Spiritual Algorithms vs. Pure Simplicity

Over-busy lives trying to *yield* to a sensitive God, is simply mission impossible for most of us! We must first ditch the busyness, *(I am talking heart and mind busyness)* because many of us are treating our relationship with God like a spiritual-algorithm that we just can't figure out!

When, in actual fact, all we have to do is slow down *(inwardly),* to be sensitive enough to recognise God when He does speak to us. And I really don't fear any contradiction when I say, it's really that simple and not an over simplification.

These are basic principles that I have used to walk out my own relationship with God, for well over 30 years now! Why would God make rocket-science of this? We don't have to reinvent the wheel. We tend to make things way too complicated, re-creating the very stumbling blocks that Christ died to remove.

Relationship First

We simply must freely enter into the abundant relationship offered us, with our Heavenly Father. **The anointing will take care of it-self!** First thing must come first. Reconciliation with the Father meant that the veil was forever torn in two. **No barrier exists, except the ones we create.**

In the very beginning we see God's Spirit and His Word inseparable. "In the beginning God created... And the Spirit of God moved... And God said..." *(Genesis 1:1-2 KJV)* Or as the Voice translation offers it: "In the beginning, God created everything... while God's Spirit hovered...Then there was the voice of God."

The Stillness of His Voice

Let's look at the following passage in 1 Kings 19:11-13 *(KJV)* where it says:

*And he said, Go forth, and stand upon the mount before the Lord. And, behold, the Lord passed by, and a great and strong wind rent the mountains, and brake in pieces the rocks before the Lord; but the Lord was NOT in the wind: and after the wind an earthquake; but the Lord was NOT in the earthquake: And after the earthquake a fire; but the Lord was NOT in the fire: and after the fire **a still small voice... Elijah heard it...***

Elijah heard it...

Probably the most potent part of this passage is the three words *"Elijah heard it."* I say this because as I shared, my precious reader is not the only one who has ever struggled to hear this *still small voice* of God. In fact because our lives are so saturated today, with all kinds of chatter *(internet, social media and/or other)*, there exists so much *commotion* in our brains! However the passage above overwhelmingly reveals that the Lord is *not in* all the commotions of life. **But He can be found in the stillness of His own voice.** Elijah heard it, but can we?

A similar scenario transpires later on in 2 Kings 2:10-12 (*KJV*), where commotion tried to rule the day again but lost:

*And he said, Thou hast asked a hard thing: nevertheless, **if thou see** me when I am taken from thee, it shall be so unto thee; but if not, it shall not be so.*

*And it came to pass, as they still went on, and talked, that, behold, there appeared a chariot of fire, and horses of fire, and parted them both asunder; and Elijah went up by a whirlwind into heaven. **And Elisha saw it,** and he cried...*

Elisha saw it...

In like fashion, probably the most potent part of this passage are the three words *"Elisha saw it..!"* Thankfully both Elijah and Elisha were not so easily distracted. Many of us would have been! Had either one of them been less disciplined, the outcome would have been radically different.

We too can alter the course of our lives, by being more sensitive to God than to our surroundings. Both Elijah and Elisha were so tuned into God, that all the chaos and kerfuffle in the world could not distract them.

Our modern-day distractions might not consist of chariots of fire per-se nonetheless ours are no less potent. Our jobs, families and other social involvements still create enough commotion in our lives to distract us from God.

Such distractions are designed to wear-us-down and blind-side us. And more often than not we reach a place where we are no longer available for God (*spiritually, emotionally or even intellectually).* **Yet He tenderly and regularly wants to speak with us.**

I use the word tenderly, because while all the distractions can be quite violent, God's voice is inward and gentle, that's why it's so easy to miss and we must tune our lives accordingly, if we really want to hear God. *Life can make us so tough, that we can no longer relate to the gentleness of God. Even Jesus had to say to His disciples one day "...ye know not what manner of spirit ye are of" (Luke 9:55 KJV).*

Hearing and Obedience Produces Fruit

And for those who say that God is *not* speaking today, I would simply suggest the contrary that God is *always* speaking. Revealed specifically in the words that Jesus taught when He said, "My sheep *hear* and *know* my voice, and I know them, *and they follow me" (John 10:27 KJV).*

The most potent part of this passage being the three little words, *"...they follow me."* "Be ye doers of the word, and not hearers only, deceiving your own selves" *(James 1:22 KJV).*

When Jesus said - *"my sheep hear... know... and follow"* - this points to obedience or as I have titled this chapter, Fearless Willingness. In fact the word *follow* is just another word for obedience! We must all be clear about this, that hearing God involves obedience. People, who say they are hearing God, yet never go to church, tithe, honour leadership *(or people in general)*, witness or ever obey His Word; I'd agree, these precious people are hearing something but it's not God!

The bible declares very clearly that, we are known by our fruit. If God is really part of our lives, our lives will produce good fruit. This involves tremendous change! *(No one who truly encounters God can ever remain the same)*. Therefore if there is zero evidence or fruit in our lives, then it seriously brings into doubt the authenticity of our relationship with God.

Even Jesus Travelled the Road to Maturity

That's why most people tend not to ask God any meaningful questions - because they dare not! They really don't want any responsibility. They don't want change. They know that hearing God equals some form of responsibility. Yet by attempting to avoid any responsibility, they make their *professed* relationship with God counter-productive and *sterile*.

Now, of course we've all had to learn *how* to distinguish God's voice from the rest! Usually it's in the very trials of this life that we learn to hear God. Jesus was not exempt from this learning process. **Even for Him maturity was a journey.** That's why I call this popular book series, "Truth for the Journey" because it's a road we must all travel.

"Though he was God's Son, **he learned trusting-obedience by what he suffered just as we do.** Then, having arrived at the full stature of his maturity... he became the source of eternal salvation to all who believingly obey him" *(Hebrews 5:8 MSG)*.

Today we are so self absorbed that we think that all the conditions must be perfect *otherwise it just cannot be God!* Well that thinking just does not line up with scripture. There was a lot of suffering going on in the scriptures. It's still often in that very place, where God can communicate with us best: **"...if indeed we share in his sufferings in order that we may also share in his glory"** *(Romans 8:17)*.

Not everyone wants to preach that. While it might not be a glamorous journey that we are called to and might require something of us *(other than being self-serving)*, most of us still have not strived for our faith, to the point of spilling our own blood. We must all know - especially here in the west - that **the absence of luxury is not suffering!**

Creating an Uninterrupted Environment

Sensing God in our environment involves creating an environment conducive with hearing His voice. We must just accept that hearing God in a crowd is doable, but is not the ideal. There is a time for everything and there are times when we must draw away from the noise and be still before God. Jesus regularly drew aside from the crowd to create that environment of stillness. His usual place of refuge was on the mountaintop.

Not because it was trending on Twitter, but because He required an uninterrupted-audience with His Heavenly Father, to get through His day! *(A developed discipline in Jesus' adult life, one that we must emulate)*. **We too need to create that space in our lives, where God can be sought and heard without interruption.**

Ejecting without Rejecting

Sure if we could simply *eliminate* all the clutter and commotion in our lives, every time we set out to pray, that would make it easier perhaps, but that's just not going to happen any time soon. None of us have managed to achieve that yet! And Jesus did not eliminate the people around Him to get intimate with His Heavenly Father. In fact Jesus' *modus operandi* was to *eject* Himself not *reject* them. In other words, He *ejected* Himself from the crowd, without rejecting the crowd.

Equally it's our responsibility to get alone with God and not blame others for crowding us from God's presence! Jesus took responsibility for His prayer life and did not blame others for the lack of it!

Vantage Point

The world will never stop spinning to let us get off! Instead Jesus knew when, where and how to separate Himself from the crowd, in order to re-enter it again - from an advantaged position - a stronger position. Prayer is a place where a divine-exchange takes place. None of us can get by without it.

> ***Those who wait*** *upon God* ***get fresh strength.*** *They spread their wings and soar like eagles, they run and* ***don't get tired,*** *they walk and* ***don't lag behind.***
>
> *(Isaiah 40:31 MSG)*

The Secret Place

There is a balance here. Both Elijah and Elisha could hear and see God in the midst of great distraction and so could Jesus. Even with the entire crowd pressing on Him, Jesus still knew that virtue had gone out of Him and had healed the woman with the issue of blood. The point is this: Jesus' sensitivity in the midst of the commotion was cultivated in that place of peace called the secret place. **We all must have a secret place. Only then can we handle the commotion.**

As we attempt to do-life, storms come and go. The house that was built on the rock still encountered storms, just as the house on the sand did *(it did not avoid the storm just because its foundations were different),* however it handled the storms better. It came out the other side.

Sometimes we think that storms and difficulty won't ever reach us. But the storms do come. It's how we prepare for them that count. Kathryn Kuhlman once said, "I live prepared!"

Peace is God's Frequency

The balance to this of course, is that we cannot become so *storm* orientated that we can never be in a place to experience *gentleness.* Our antenna must be tuned into God no matter what's going on around us. How do we recognise His frequency? **God's frequency is always peace.** We know this, because Jesus is described as the Prince of Peace. He is not the author of confusion or chaos, *(we create our own mess!)* So although He might not have authored the storms in your life, He certainly creates the peace in the midst of every storm! "Thou wilt keep him in **perfect peace,** whose mind is stayed on thee…" *(Isaiah 26:3 KJV)*

Learning to be Available

"Step out of the traffic! Take a long, loving look at me… above politics, above everything" *(Psalm 46:10 MSG).* There is something powerful about being still, that enables us to hear God. Inward peace *(regardless of our surroundings)* is the only place where we are going to hear God. **Peace makes us available to Him.**

This then must be our ultimate goal in life, to cultivate the kind of peace that allows us to hear God's voice in the midst of life. Intimate "stillness" is required of us. The fruit of which is knowledge... the growing knowledge of Him. *"Be still and know that I am God" (Psalm 46:10 KJV).* "Be still, *be calm, see,* and understand I am the True God" *(AMP).*

The original language includes the contexts: *let drop; relax.* So many times in my life, God has issued me this instruction, *"Let go and let Me."* Why? Because letting go means letting Him! *(It's important we get out of the way).*

Many times when we come to God in prayer, we are so stressed out, that being *still* becomes mission impossible. It's only possible, when we let go. Let go of all that we think we know, and know God better instead. The original language involves the words: *to recognise, acknowledge and diligence.*

Knowing God is continually letting go and *acknowledging* His presence in our everyday lives and circumstances. Being *diligent* in cultivating a relationship with Him where we can *recognise* Him in all situations. Having the ability to discern what God *isn't* doing can be just as important, same way Jesus told His disciples that calling down fire on a village was not the right move - nor was it the right spirit!

Gentleness and Greatness go Hand in Hand

When it comes to *letting go and letting God,* the word to *yield* is a good interpretation here. Although *yielding* to God doesn't come naturally and we must seek the help of the

Holy Spirit. *Yielding* might seem too *passive* for some people. Yet it empowered Jesus, who walked on water!

So let's learn to *ride* the storms of life rather than *yield* to them! To serve the One who can be found in the midst of them and where every confused-emotion must bow its knee to the presence of God, where only the fullness of joy can dwell!

So it's time to relax and trust God, because in all of our striving we can actually miss God completely! This means that even though He is omni-present *(always present)* we still manage to miss Him because we have not developed sensitivity towards His presence and His voice. This involves being incredibly gentle. **And did you know that gentleness and greatness go hand in hand?**

Power-Under-Control

The best example of this would be God Himself, Who is fiercely powerful and yet incredibly gentle, simultaneously. Think of gentleness as being *power-under-control!* David knew this concept because he wrote the words of Psalms 18:35 *"... your gentleness has made me great"* (KJV), on the same day that God delivered him from the hand of Saul.

In addition to this, Derek Prince once shared how he had fallen asleep just as his plane was landing on the runway. He marvelled how such a huge piece of machinery could be so gentle, to the point that it didn't wake him up, another great example of power-under-control.

However there is none more *powerfully gentle* than God Himself, Who wants to manifests both His *gentleness* and *power* in our lives. **Religion denied of its power, is useless. Equally power without gentleness is dangerous.** What balance that creates!

Closer than Breath

So going back to the person who wrote to me, I do believe that people often try too hard "to *come* to God," instead of just relaxing in His presence. The emphasis has to be on *yielding* to God, not *striving* towards Him. Why? Because God's closer than our own breath, we must learn to yield to Him; the rest will take care of itself!

I don't want to over simplify this here, but I do want you to know that only a *religious spirit* wants you to keep *striving* for God's presence, when you already have it! A religious spirit wants you always tangled up in religious rituals, methods and systems – so that you're always striving to come to God. But the veil was torn in two. There's no obstacle anymore.

Every Single Day!

This has long been my simple philosophy and as a result, I experience the presence of God every single day of my life. It's really not that difficult. God went to great lengths to make a way when there was none in order to reconcile us, through the finished work of the cross. So why then would He continue to make this hard for us, when He longs to be with us?

So finally this *stillness* that we both want and need is only achievable with the help of the Holy Spirit. But let's not forget that sin, which is disobedience, brings separation between God and us. However 1 John 1:9 tells us that, "If we confess our sins, he is faithful and just to forgive us our sins…" *(NKJV)* So we must not hesitate to surrender our sins/burdens to God, so that we can enjoy an unfettered relationship with Him. After all, He desires unhindered proximity, more than we do!

> ***Draw near to God and He will draw near to you.***
> *(James 4:8 NKJV)*

❖

CHAPTER 8

Obedience brings Prosperity

It is His faith in us alone that can accomplish the
destiny to which He has set before us!

...by the faith OF the Son of God.
(Galatians 2:20 KJV)

Some years ago within the early years of my ministry,
a time when I was seeking the Lord to use me. Earnestly
praying and seeking God's face, like many young men I
really wanted to do everything that God had called me to do.

I loved hearing stories of the saints of old who down
through the ages etched their mark on history, as we know
it. I have always been inspired to read about their small
beginnings and how God took them from nothing and made
a something out of them!

Potent

Smith Wigglesworth was such a man, simple in speech, unsophisticated, and a true man's-man, whom I could relate to. Regardless of education or eloquence, he was potent for the Lord!

These types were my inspiration and I remember one day, crying out to God, "If only I could be like Smith Wigglesworth." To which I remember God's reply as if it were only yesterday, **"Why limit yourself?"** At first not understanding, I soon realised what He was communicating: **"Don't be bound by another man's achievements. Take your eyes off of men and get them back on Me."**

God never requires us to clone ourselves nor strive to fulfil another man's destiny. In fact it's only as we keep our eyes on Him to hear His guiding voice, will we possess faith sufficient enough to fulfil our own divine destiny without limit.

Living by the Faith of the Son of God

Long ago I realised this simple but life changing truth, superseding all my prior best efforts: ample is faith all the time that we yield our lives to "the faith of the Son of God." Trying to muster our own faith can be pitiful! No! "I live," Paul said in Galatians 2:20, "by the faith of the Son of God."

I am crucified with Christ: nevertheless I live; yet not I, but Christ liveth in me: and the life which I now live in the flesh I live by the faith of the Son of God, who loved me, and gave himself for me.

(Galatians 2:20 KJV)

Through yielding we not only have sufficient faith *in* but also enjoy the faith *of* the Son of God. It is His faith in us alone that can accomplish the destiny to which He has set before us!

> *And I am convinced and sure of this very thing, that He Who began a good work in you will continue until the day of Jesus Christ [right up to the time of His return], developing [that good work] and perfecting and bringing it to full completion in you.*
>
> *(Philippians 1:6 AMP)*

My prayer for you, precious reader is that you not only study to show yourself approved, but that you earnestly look to God for the path which He has set before you. Yielding to His faith that never stops reaching for your destiny, in full obedience.

Hearing God

My heart aches whenever I think of all the wasted potential in the world today, staggering millions of people with talents untapped, underdeveloped and un-applauded.

Others choose to live far below their potential and talents in the spirit of fear and procrastination. Listen, no one appreciates an educated fool or even an expert who is really only someone who knows everything about something and nothing else! People don't much care for the educated guess either. What cuts the ice is our ability to hear God and live out those instructions with **fearless willingness.**

> *He who is able to hear, let him listen to and give heed to what the Spirit says to the assemblies (churches). To*

him who overcomes (is victorious), I will grant to eat [of
the fruit] of the tree of life, which is in the paradise of God.
(Revelation 2:7 AMP)

In the last 30+ years of walking with the Lord I have seen much success simply by obeying God's voice. This doesn't negate knowing his written Word of course! Nevertheless relationship without Rhema is a misnomer or an oxymoron!

Allowing God to Use You

In the process of time, I have also seen many go through systems of education, with great earnest, endeavour and expectation only to come out the other side fully equipped with qualifications they never use! Many fail to step beyond the preparation and allow God to use them to the max.

Our intelligence and education surrounding the Word of God must never cease to be paramount, but **one must never substitute obedience for knowledge alone.** Yet the process of equipping us with skill in the things of God is only to aid our obedience to His voice. Rightly dividing His Word in the spirit of revelation has its purpose buried in the fact that we ought to live obediently to the now Word of God, knowing how to walk in resurrection life!

My encouragement for anyone studying in preparation for what God has said is this: **In all your pursuit of knowledge, never fail to develop a hearing ear.** And in the hearing, is the doing!

Sadly a relatively small percentage of all students ever end up doing what they actually studied for. My prayer is that you not only fulfil your potential and purpose but also to *walk* it through to completion.

The Apostle Paul said,

> *For we are his workmanship, created in Christ Jesus unto good works, which God hath before ordained **that we should walk in them.***
>
> *(Ephesians 2:10 KJV)*

It's evident that God assigned a special path in life for you. **It is your duty to find out what that path is and walk it through, with the Faith of the Son of God.**

Fifth Pillar
CONNECTIONS

❖

CHAPTER 9

A Network of Relationships

As we share this journey and discover these seven pillars of life, let me begin in this chapter by saying that one of the signs of the times, in reference to what the Holy Spirit is doing, is that He continually orchestrates divine connections that produce strong relationships, which in turn develops Kingdom business.

> Do you have any **spiritual relationships?** ...having the same attitude and the same love, living in harmony, and keeping one purpose in mind...
>
> (Philippians 2:1-2 GW)

It is important to state that without *networking* in regards to ministry, there would be little growth. For this very reason the Holy Spirit is directing us to continually focus on building relationships so that a strong *net* is produced, a *network* of relationships, which productively interact for God's Kingdom.

End Time Apostolic Fishing Nets

Such a network of relationships is *apostolic,* something that the Holy Spirit is fully engaged in and will continue to develop for the end time move of God.

These relationships look for apostolic support and encouragement from other men and women of God in order to move forwards boldly and powerfully in the Holy Spirit. This is where they are properly released to fulfil their destinies.

Network literally means: *a linking of people with a common interest or area of concern.* Therefore as we move on in this millennium we will see continued emphasis on and the development of such networks, which are willing to work together interdenominational, via association. Networking does not imply that all groups should come under some pope-like-figure or one apostolic movement.

Corporate Visions and Powerful Knots

Quite simply *networking* implies associations or groups who work together like a powerful *fishing net.* Each member of a network representing one of the **knots** that helps tie the net together. Those who have vision, grace and wisdom, to network with other networks will become the great fishing net that God will use to draw in the great multitude of souls.

Dr. Bill Hamon says of such networks, "This gives the Holy Spirit the opportunity to bring a greater unity and corporate vision within the Body of Christ. This will enable all available resources to be harnessed to work together towards assisting the Body of Christ to initiate and sustain an effective thrust towards souls. The common meeting ground is to have the corporate vision of reaping the great end time harvest and proclaiming Jesus Christ as Lord over all the earth" (Hamon 14).

Kingdom Dragnets

In the Amplified Version it aptly refers to a *dragnet* here in Matthew 13:47, "Again, the kingdom of heaven is like a dragnet which was cast into the sea and gathered in fish of every sort."

The Message Bible on the other hand calls it a "fishnet" where the Authorised Version simply uses the word "net," which in the Greek refers to a fishing net but also to a *pack-saddle (which in the East was merely a bag of **netted** rope)* but interestingly the root meaning for "net" actually means "to equip!" *(see Strong's #G4522)* Also see the following scriptures: Matthew 4:19; 9:35; 13:49; John 21:1-ff; James 3:13; 4:1-8; 1 Peter 5:5-10.

Effectively, a network depends upon people *(pastors and ministers)* who are totally committed in every aspect of their life to the Lord Jesus Christ; who are willing to use their God given talents and abilities without regard to the cost, with great joy. Remembering that this relationship of association networking is not to threaten or contradict denominational loyalties or cause division but to help bring strength, depth, unity, clarity, and the Word of God that can only enhance better skills and insights into sharing God's Word.

Spiritual Hubs of Government

One of the aims of a network is as follows: to help establish ministry centres of excellence and significance for this present move of God. *"Spiritual Hubs of Government"* enhance God's Kingdom and provide a "platform" *(for ministry gifts)* to speak into cities and nations in an effective way.

To develop ministries, enhancing and bringing them into positions of leadership, to influence every area of society. To combine their skills, experience and abilities, to make increasing individual and corporate impact in the regions of their influence for the Kingdom of God and for the Glory of the Lord Jesus Christ.

Lastly let's take a closer look at the purpose of knots: we could say that divine appointments are like "knots" in a net. They are strong connections that can take the strain and bombardments of teamwork or apostolic relationships. In other words each person is a knot; the net is only as strong as each *knot* or *connection*. **Knots bring certain stabilising features that help empower the net;** the same is true of the Kingdom such as strength, ability, security, prosperity, healing, unity, harmony and trust.

Facts about Nets

Fact: Fishermen spend a great portion of their time mending and cleaning their nets; perhaps more time than actually fishing! Equally we must spend larger portions of our time on relationships that will help develop the Kingdom, *(His net)*. In this way we will be more effective.

Fact: When used to catch fish, dragnets see a large percentage of what is caught, thrown directly back into the sea *(for being either the wrong type or wrong size)*. Likewise we too will catch *undesirable* things in our net at times.

In addition consider this, **God is looking for fish that can be gutted!** In other words, those who are not ready to *give* themselves are thrown back as rejects... but those who can be *processed* and *prepared* are kept!

The Kingdom of Heaven is like a Net

Our emphasis here is evidently the "Kingdom of God" just as Matthew 13:47 clearly stated; **"the kingdom of heaven is like a net..."** This was a direct teaching about the Kingdom not a net; but parallels are drawn and the net is used as a metaphor. However certain characteristics about the Kingdom can be deduced based on our knowledge of nets.

I will close by saying that the Kingdom of God involves the following: the restoration of the net equals the establishing, strengthening and maintenance of robust Kingdom relationships. Each knot has to work together to make the whole net viable. As the knots *(apostolic connections)* submit to one another in love, this makes the net *(Kingdom)* more effective.

Final conclusion: True apostolic networking best represents God's Kingdom on this earth. We must therefore be willing to work together multilaterally *(and internationally)*, to be steered by the agenda of the Holy Spirit, for the Kingdom of God.

❖

CHAPTER 10

Principles of Wise Relationships

In the recent decades I have been bringing leaders together, in different countries, under the banner of *Connecting for Excellence,* a platform for gathering leaders from all over the globe. CFE is where leaders connect and tie knots for the greater good, the overall dragnet of God's Kingdom worldwide where lasting relationships are established in an obligation free environment.

I've found that everyone is looking for the right relationships *(potent connections)*, especially leaders. It matters little whether they're seasoned in the ministry or just starting out. Some already have their own established circles of influence and others have none, but they are still looking for more.

Leaders of every kind thrive best when they can *gather, connect* and *build* collaborating and mutual relationships *(covenantal friendships)* that have impact around the world.

CFE is a God given vision that supports leaders and provides a forum for divine appointments to be made that enhances Kingdom development in their respective countries.

Why is it important to Build Relationships First?

Dr. Robb Thompson says the following, "As I reviewed life, I looked for one common thread, and discovered that there is one thing that seems to be present in all of its many facets, *relationships.*

- *All good comes from relationships*
- *All evil has its roots in relationships*

I pondered and wanted to discover what the things I wanted to avoid were and what things that I needed to make certain were present in all of them to guarantee their success.

At any given time there are three distinct people in your life:

- **The Compromiser:** is always trying to get you to compromise your standards... past friends; acquaintances
- **The Companion:** those whose influence is neither good nor bad for your future, at least not yet (*friends, family, the fun people, but take you nowhere*)
- **The Committed:** those who are undoubtedly committed to your success (*but those we usually take for granted*)

Principles of Wise Relationships

Relationships are magnetic, pulling you closer to or driving you further away from your divine destiny.

He who walks with the wise grows wise, but a companion of fools suffers harm.

(Proverbs 13:20)

A righteous man is cautious in friendship, but the way of the wicked leads them astray.

(Proverbs 12:26)

Genuine relationships are never defined by what we can get, but by what we can give. We must always be careful to make certain that we deposit more into the relationship than what we withdraw. This is what gives it longevity *(long life, prolonged existence, permanence, durability, endurance).*

Love must be sincere. Hate what is evil; cling to what is good.

(Romans 12:9)

Be devoted to one another in brotherly love. Honour one another above yourselves.

(Romans 12:10)

Do to others as you would have them do to you.

(Luke 6:31)

In everything I did, I showed you that by this kind of hard work we must help the weak, remembering the words the Lord Jesus himself said: "It is more blessed to give than to receive."

(Acts 20:35)

Do nothing out of selfish ambition or vain conceit, but in humility consider others better than yourselves.

(Philippians 2:3)

You cannot go to the next level without friendship, relationships and without the Body of Christ. If you want to accurately predict a man's future, just take a look at his present friends.

You are my friends if you do what I command.

(John 15:14)

Requirements for Relationship

- My friends must be committed to their families, husbands/wives *(1 Timothy 3:1-8)*

- My friends must be committed to long lasting relationships. I have had to bring some relationships to a close. In ministry one of the biggest problems I find with ministry friends is an Absalom spirit, gaining information that gives power. This is when one thinks he has an ordained position because he has access to information

- My friends must have empires in their brains *(people of vision, who do not mock me for dreaming big)*

- My friends must be sowers, they want to support because they see the spiritual implications

- My friends must qualify to receive my seed, they qualify by understanding seedtime and harvest

- My friends must prize integrity above relationship *(integrity means completeness, prosperity, innocence, fullness, uprightness at a venture. It also carries the meaning of being whole, upright, made perfect and entire, lacking nothing)*

• My friends must be willing to confront my enemies; my friends must stop those who speak negatively about me/family or ministry. And certainly not enter or speak negatively themselves in regard to their relationship with me

What you desire in life is guaranteed the moment you grant it. Many cannot sustain lasting relationships *(this is true of ministers)* because they are coveting to gain opportunity to be able to *(in their thinking)* develop somehow their so-called ministry.

Ephesians 4:11-13 speaks of the apostolic in regard to preparing others for service, so that the Body of Christ may be built up until we all reach unity in the faith and in the knowledge of the Son of God and become mature, attaining to the whole measure of the fullness of Christ.

Those who are well established in ministry should stop looking for opportunities to gain more pundits but to help by serving others through encouragement to develop and fulfil their divine destiny. Especially those who are in some business venture etc., I am personally against pyramid selling.

Because you know that the Lord will reward everyone for whatever good he does, whether he is slave or free.
(Ephesians 6:8)

Do to others as you would have them do to you.

(Luke 6:31)

When he had finished washing their feet, he put on his clothes and returned to his place. "Do you understand what I have done for you?" he asked them. "You call me 'Teacher' and 'Lord,' and rightly so, for that is what I am. Now that I, your Lord and Teacher, have washed your feet, you also should wash one another's feet."

(John 13:12-14)

I have set you an example that you should do as I have done for you.

(John 13:15)

Whose future are you helping to Create?

The future of the student is guaranteed the moment he creates one *(a future)* for his teacher.

Do not be deceived: God cannot be mocked. A man reaps what he sows. The one who sows to please his sinful nature [his wants], from that nature will reap destruction; the one who sows to please the Spirit, from the Spirit will reap eternal life.

Let us not become weary in doing good, for at the proper time we will reap a harvest if we do not give up.

(Galatians 6:7-9)

A wise servant will rule over a disgraceful **son, and will share the inheritance as one of the brothers.**

(Proverbs 17:2)

A life without a harvest is proof that you have lived it with the wrong people.

Give, and it will be given to you. A good measure, pressed down, shaken together and running over, will be poured into your lap. For with the measure you use, it will be measured to you.

(Luke 6:38)

Finally use *time* as a Sifter

You will never trust anything that *time* has not tested. You will need *time* to show you what your discernment couldn't. You will never know who someone really is until you use *time* to go beyond their appearance. *Time* reveals information that words tried to cover up. Your emotions need *time* to be enlightened by information" (Thompson).

Sixth Pillar

MANAGEMENT

❖

CHAPTER 11

Overcoming Crisis Through Kingdom Management

In this chapter and sixth pillar we are looking at the subject of Kingdom Management, which I believe is a crucial concept. Without sound management in our lives, everything is handed over to anarchy and chaos, of which God is not the author, "For God is not the author of confusion, but of **peace**… " (1 Corinthians 14:33 KJV)

The word *peace,* which is shalom in Hebrew and *eirene* in Greek means: *completeness, health, soundness, welfare, perfect (nothing missing or broken); security, safety, prosperity (see Strong's #H7965; #G1515).*

So in a nutshell, peace in our lives is a result of good management.

The Management of the Holy Spirit

The Holy Spirit gets to work on our chaos the moment we are born again! He will not cohabit with chaos. Therefore if we are to host the presence of God, we must allow Him to work on our lives: "Don't you know that **your body is the temple of the Holy Spirit** who comes from God and dwells inside of you? You do not own yourself. You have been **purchased at a great price,** so use your body to **bring glory to God!**" *(1 Corinthians 6:19-20 VOICE)*

Quite frankly, chaos does not glorify God! And like you perhaps, I came to God, a-walking-mess! I needed His order in my life. I may have been a willing recipient but that doesn't imply that gaining control over my chaos came easily for me - no way!

God's Change Agent

It was years *(and with much deliverance)* before God's order began to reign sovereign in my heart and in my actions. I simply couldn't remain the same. I had to change. We all have to change. We can come as we are and be accepted - but then we must change, in fact it's impossible to stay the same. The Holy Spirit is God's change agent!

Now, chaos might be all *around* us but it must not be *in* us! So we must yield to the change. Then as each storm comes, we don't mutate or become part of the storm, instead we overcome! Understand something today - you were designed to overcome. Jesus did not eject us. He left us here, to overcome, and that is what we must do. **We have an unbeatable spirit, winning is in our nature!**

He that OVERCOMETH shall inherit ALL THINGS;
and I will be his God, and he shall be my son.

(Revelation 21:7 KJV)

Overcoming

While living in Italy, there was one word that obsessed the people: *crisi (crisis!)* It was like the chorus that ended *every* conversation and news-real. The media were gripped by the struggling economy *(crisieconomica)*. But Italy has never really been famous for its sound-management, rather for corruption, especially in the area of politics. *(The system is burdensomely bureaucratic and you can easily get tangled in red tape there, if you don't know how to navigate!)* Italians generally don't trust their government - *politicians* in particular.

Another European country that has made headlines in recent times for its apparent lack of economic management is Greece. Which has all put pressure on the Euro and is something that sophisticated Germany who has yet again, emerged as the powerhouse of Europe, remains not too pleased about.

So let's say that most crises, especially those economic in nature, result from mismanagement: fear, a lack of knowledge and greed.

The Kingdom of Heaven Defined

We see this in Matthew chapter 25, where two parables are given to describe what the Kingdom of God will be like.

While the first parable focuses on ten virgins *(and what could be perceived as the mismanagement of **time**)*, the second parable focuses on the grievous mismanagement of money.

As follows:

> *At that time the kingdom of heaven will be like... a man going on a journey, who called his servants and **entrusted his wealth to them.** To one he gave five bags of gold, to another two bags, and to another one bag, **each according to his ability.** Then he went on his journey. The man who had received five bags of gold went **at once and put his money to work** and gained five bags more. So also, the one with two bags of gold gained two more. **But the man who had received one bag went off, dug a hole in the ground and hid his master's money.***

> *After a long time the master of those servants returned and settled accounts with them. The man who had received five bags of gold brought the other five. "Master," he said, "you entrusted me with five bags of gold. See, I have gained five more." His master replied, **"Well done, good and faithful servant! You have been faithful with a few things; I will put you in charge of many things.** Come and share your master's happiness!"*

> *The man with two bags of gold also came. "Master," he said, "you entrusted me with two bags of gold; see, I have gained two more." His master replied, **"Well done, good and faithful servant! You have been faithful with a few things; I will put you in charge of many things.** Come and share your master's happiness!"*

*Then the man who had received one bag of gold came. "Master," he said, "I knew that you are a hard man, harvesting where you have not sown and gathering where you have not scattered seed. **So I was afraid and went out and hid your gold in the ground. See, here is what belongs to you."***

*His master replied, **"You wicked, lazy servant!** So you knew that I harvest where I have not sown and gather where I have not scattered seed? Well then, you should have put my money on deposit with the bankers, so that when I returned I would have received it back with interest."*

"So take the bag of gold from him and give it to the one who has ten bags. For whoever has will be given more, and they will have an abundance. Whoever does not have, even what they have will be taken from them. And throw that worthless servant outside, into the darkness, where there will be weeping and gnashing of teeth."

(Matthew 25:1; 14-30)

Fear Kills Productivity & Accuses God

Faith goes into effect *immediately;* fear procrastinates. The scripture above states that, "The man who had received five bags of gold **went *at once* and put his money to work** and gained five bags more." His fearless demeanour produced much fruit and without difficulty.

However the servant who operated out of fear was much less fruitful. In fact his master didn't take too kindly to being falsely accused by this "wicked and lazy servant," who not only accused him of being a "hard man" but of steeling no less! "Harvesting where you have not sown and gathering where you have not scattered..."

So why did this servant behave so differently to the other servants? The obvious answer is FEAR! "I was *afraid* and went out and *hid* your gold in the ground. See, here is what belongs to you." Fear causes us to *mismanage* what is placed in our charge:

- When we strive instead of thrive - fear is present
- When we become threatened and suspicious - fear is present
- When we are non-productive - fear is present
- When dreams and goals are aborted – fear is present
- When there's a lack of breakthrough – fear is present
- Where there's a lack of provision – fear is present
- When there's a lack of joy and victory – fear is present

We must never operate out of fear - it is a totally wrong spirit *(see 2 Timothy 1:7)*. Fear causes poor judgment and results in poor management. "Wicked and lazy servants" refuse to take responsibility and prefer taking the safer position of judging, criticising and accusing others, *(including God!)*

In Christ, we have been called to be good and faithful servants who are faithful with few things, so that we can be put in charge of many *(see Matthew 25:21)*.

Crisis Management

What kind of crisis are you facing right now? Perhaps if you trace it back to its beginning, you'll discover that mismanagement and greed are at its core? Perhaps you've been the victim of someone else's greed and mismanagement, even if not your own?

For example we can see in today's economy, that it's always the poor who suffer the most, from the greed of others. When the big banks got greedy and made their mistakes, they got bailed out and just carried on as usual, the fat cats still received their fat bonuses. But it's the low-income folks, who are still footing the bill! This bites... especially when the banks play it safe - they don't have to suffer the consequences of their mismanagement and greed - yet everyone else must!

Take Courage Jesus has Overcome the World!

A crisis will make you a victim if you are not careful. The mess might not have been your fault, but you can control your *coming-out*. In the same context, **you might not have chosen the hand you were dealt, but you can choose how you play it!**

Here is a short list of some of the complex emotions experienced from crisis: worry, self pity, depression, dread *(fear of loss)*, misery, discouragement, defeatism, fatalism *(especially joblessness)*, negativity, cynicism, brooding loneliness, grieving, frustration, anxiety, despair and hopelessness, self-hate, humiliation, demoralisation, and **in some cases unresolved trauma.** This can go on to develop abandonment issues, fear of death and obsessive-self-preservation *(paranoia)*.

In spite of all this, any crisis can and *must* be overcome. Jesus did not pull any punches because He openly warned us about the ongoing crisis in this world:

> *...in this godless world you will continue to experience difficulties.*
>
> *(John 16:33 MSG)*

> *...in the world ye shall have dis-ease.*
>
> *(John 16:33 WYC)*

> *...many trials and sorrows.*
>
> *(John 16:33 NLT)*

> *...plagued with times of trouble.*
>
> *(John 16:33 VOICE)*

However if our foundation is the Solid-Rock of Christ *(and not sand)* we can go through any storm: "Trust in the Lord *(commit yourself to Him, lean on Him, hope confidently in Him)* forever; for the Lord God is an everlasting Rock [the **Rock of Ages**]" *(Isaiah 26:4 AMP)*.

We'll still experience storms - no matter how well insulated we think our lives are - one after the other! The point is learning how to overcome and recover from the storms - not analyse them! In Christ we are over-comers and the book of Revelation gives this mighty assurance: **"HE THAT OVERCOMETH SHALL INHERIT ALL THINGS..."** *(Revelation 21:7 KJV)*

Christ is our Leverage

If we don't manage ourselves, the crisis will manage us. Then all sorts of negative things can start happening. For example individuals, who aren't coping with life, resort to all manner of coping mechanisms: alcohol and drug abuse, obesity and bulimia, sexual deviancy, the occult and many other practices of physical, psychological, even spiritual mismanagement.

On the extreme end of the scale, some people even become psychotic *(severely mentally ill and deranged)*. Yet Jesus said, **"...but be of good cheer [take courage; be confident, certain, undaunted]! For I have overcome the world. [I have deprived it of power to harm you and have conquered it for you]"** *(John 16:33 AMP).*

> *In all these things we are more than conquerors through him who loved us.* For I am convinced that neither death nor life, neither angels nor demons, neither the present nor the future, nor any powers, neither height nor depth, nor anything else in all creation, will be able to separate us from the love of God that is in **Christ Jesus our Lord.**
>
> *(Romans 8:37-39)*

There is no alternative to Christ. Short-lived victories that some people seem to enjoy in this life will not last forever: "Don't bother your head with braggarts or wish you could succeed like the wicked. In no time they'll shrivel like grass clippings and wilt like cut flowers in the sun..." *(Psalm 37:1-2 MSG)*

Measure Success with Christ not the Culture

Take your everyday, ordinary life - your sleeping, eating, going-to-work, and walking-around life - and place it before God as an offering. Embracing what God does for you is the best thing you can do for him. **Don't become so well-adjusted to your culture that you fit into it without even thinking.**

Instead, fix your attention on God. You'll be changed from the inside out. Readily recognize what he wants from you, and quickly respond to it. **Unlike the culture around you, always dragging you down to its level of immaturity, God brings the best out of you,** *develops well-formed maturity in you.*

(Romans 12:1 MSG)

Greed Motivates Mismanagement

This element plays havoc with our ability to manage; greed is so hazardous and menacing.

According to Myles Munroe greed is, "...the mismanagement of resources for personal benefit, coupled with a disregard for the benefit of others. Greed is when you want more than you need at the *expense* of everybody else" (Munroe 19).

You can be sure of this: No one will have a place in the kingdom of Christ and of God who sins sexually, or does evil things, or is greedy. **Anyone who is greedy is serving a false god.**

(Ephesians 5:5 NCV)

The definition of greed in the English language according to the Merriam-Webster Dictionary is: *"a selfish and excessive desire for more of something (as money) than is needed."*

Snared by our own Lust

The Greek definition for *greed* is: *covetousness (#G4124).* Covetous basically means: *an intense desire for things that you don't currently posses, especially things belonging to someone else.*

In Amos 3:3 it says, "Can two walk together, except they be agreed?" *(KJV)* Greed also has many unholy alliances, such as those named in Mark 7:21-22, "For it is from within, out of a person's heart, that evil thoughts come - sexual immorality, theft, murder, adultery, *greed,* malice, deceit, lewdness, envy, slander, arrogance and folly."

Greed is synonymous with lust and covetousness: "Every man is tempted, when he is drawn away of his own **lust,** and enticed" *(James 1:14 KJV).* The Wycliffe Bible uses the word covet, "Each man is tempted, drawn and stirred of his own **coveting**... drawn from reason, and snared, or deceived." The Message Bible is different again: "The temptation to give in to evil comes from us and only us. We have no one to blame but the leering, seducing flare-up of our own **lust.**"

The Importance of Heart Management

Managing our hearts *(and mouths)* is not just a case of weeding an inner garden full of weeds *(wrong thoughts);* it's much more than that. "Above all else, *guard (govern, manage)* your heart, for everything you do flows from it" *(Proverbs*

4:23). Greed is a condition of the heart and we must govern our hearts well. Hebrew for *guarding* your heart means: *"to watch over, keep, preserve, guard from dangers, guard with fidelity, keep secret, to be kept close, be blockaded" (Strong's #H5341).*

High Maintenance

In addition, about the heart Jeremiah said, "The heart is deceitful *above all things,* and *desperately wicked..." (17:9 KJV)* Without Christ we cannot contend with our own hearts, *(high maintenance is an understatement!)*

Our hearts have a lot to answer for: "...of the abundance of the heart his mouth speaketh" *(Luke 6:45 KJV).* It's our words that are the dead-give-away. They reveal the contents of our heart, and **it's the unmanaged contents of our hearts that defile us:** "The things that come out of your mouth - your curses, your fears, your denunciations - these come from your heart, and it is the stirrings of your heart that can make you unclean" *(Matthew 15:18 VOICE).*

It takes more than human effort. It takes *supernatural management* to govern the human heart. "I am the One who relentlessly explores the mind and heart, and I will deal with each of you as you deserve according to your acts" *(Revelation 2:23 VOICE);* "...appearances don't impress me. I x-ray every motive..." *(MSG)*

Individual Accountability

We have to clean up our act. We all fail constantly and have to exercise damage control, especially for all those conversations we got into that we wish we hadn't! To make things worse, according to Matthew 12:36 we're going to be held accountable for every idle word: "...people will be called to account for every careless word they have ever said" *(VOICE);* "...for every empty word" *(NIV).*

> *It's your heart, not the dictionary that gives meaning to your words...* **Every one of these careless words is going to come back to haunt you.** *There will be a time of Reckoning.* **Words are powerful; take them seriously.** *Words can be your salvation. Words can also be your damnation.*
>
> *(Matthew 12:34-37 MSG)*

The Leaking Faucet of Human Nature!

Our mouths get carried away and leak all kinds of unwanted information. We've all lived in fear of our own mouths before - let's be honest! James 3:6 says that the tongue is a world of trouble: "The tongue also is a fire, a world of evil among the parts of the body. It corrupts the whole body, sets the whole course of one's life on fire, and is itself set on fire by hell." Our tongues often speak for the fallen nature, even more reason to yield that member to the Holy Spirit and His divine nature.

> *It only takes a spark, remember, to set off a forest fire. A careless or wrongly placed word out of your mouth can do that.* **By our speech we can ruin the world, turn harmony to chaos, throw mud on a reputation,** *send the whole world up in smoke and go up in smoke with it, smoke right from the pit of hell.*
>
> *(James 3:5-6 MSG)*

Willing and Pliable Enough?

However, we can talk all day about being good managers but not everyone is willing to be *managed*. We must be teachable and pliable if we're to stay on the Potter's wheel as He uses others, such as leadership and parents, to help mould and manage our lives.

The true Body of Christ requires divine administration and so do our individual lives. There's no detail of our lives that the Holy Spirit can't grasp, especially as He numbers every hair on our heads! He governs well, all that's yielded to His control. He must be able to say to us, "You're not in the driver's seat; **I am**" *(Matthew 16:24 MSG)*.

Managing Appetites!

Human nature is subject to many appetites *(lusts)*, which must be recognised and managed properly, if we want to serve God correctly. Let's take for example, an appetite for fame and glory *(not just chocolate)!* This can steer people off course for a lifetime. None of us however, can manage appetites that we're in denial of! We must know them - to be able to manage them!

For example insecurity is an appetite. The need *(greed)* for acceptance, for attention and appreciation *(popularity)* can lead us out of the very will of God. "Envy and slander represent a greed for reputation" (Munroe 20). We must not be given to selfish appetites on any level.

Fasting helps Subdue Unruly Appetites

This is where fasting becomes relevant, in order to help us subdue such appetites. We must put off their constant nagging, **"...let us strip off and throw aside every encumbrance** (*unnecessary weight*) and that sin which so readily (*deftly and cleverly*) clings to and entangles us... Looking away [from all that will distract] to Jesus" (*Hebrews 12:1-2 AMP*).

Jesus warned against greed most clearly, **"Guard yourselves and keep free from all covetousness** (*the immoderate desire for wealth, the greedy longing to have more);* for a man's life does not consist in and is not derived from possessing overflowing abundance or that which is over and above his needs" (*Luke 12:15-21 AMP*).

Focus on Heavenly Assets

Jesus continued with this parable about greed:

A wealthy man owned some land that produced a huge harvest. He often thought to himself, "I have a problem here. I don't have anywhere to store all my crops. What should I do? I know! I'll tear down my small barns and build even bigger ones, and then I'll have plenty of storage space for my grain and all my other goods.

Then I'll be able to say to myself, 'I have it made! I can relax and take it easy for years! So I'll just sit back, eat, drink, and have a good time!'" Then God interrupted the man's conversation with himself. "Excuse Me, Mr. Brilliant, but

your time has come. Tonight you will die. Now who will enjoy everything you've earned and saved?" **This is how it will be for people who accumulate huge assets for themselves but have no assets in relation to God.**
(Luke 12:17-21 VOICE)

The Consequence of Poor Management

Poor management has a lot to answer for. On too many occasions, a crisis is the result of someone's greed: "Too much of the time, by default, people let their greed rule their decisions. They do not think about what they are doing. Down the road, their greedy decisions result in a crisis. In a crisis, not only do other people get hurt, often the greedy ones do, too" (Munroe 23).

Greed and generosity are polar opposites. In the parable above Jesus taught us that it's not possible to live for self and for God at the same time: "That's what happens when you fill your barn with Self and not with God" *(verse 21 MSG)*. It's hard to fill a cup that's already full, so I say this - we must be spilled before we can be filled.

David's Ability to Manage Well

When we look at David pursuing his enemy to get his stuff back *(including wives and children)* we know that he was not a passive leader who lead from the rear. Neither was David greedy. He managed the spoils of war righteously so that everyone got their share and he did not allow it to be hoarded wickedly.

*David came to the 200 men who were so **exhausted and faint** that they could not follow [him] and had been left at the brook Besor [with the baggage]. They came to meet David and those with him, and when he came near to the men, he saluted them. **Then all the wicked and base men** who went with David said, Because they did not go with us, we will give them nothing of the spoil we have recovered, except that every man may lead away his wife and children and depart.*

*David said, **You shall not do so, my brethren, with what the Lord has given us.** He has preserved us and has delivered into our hands the troop that came against us... **For as is the share of him who goes into the battle, so shall his share be who stays by the baggage. They shall share alike.** And from that day to this he made it a statute and ordinance for Israel.*

(1 Samuel 30:20-25 AMP)

Not So Easily Corrupted

This is a perfect example of a good leader who knew how to manage his affairs well. Meaning that everyone benefited, not just the few. There was generosity and correct distribution. King David displayed no greed at all, in his actions. **In fact leaders, parents, husbands who are motivated by greed, are easily corrupted:** "When the righteous are in authority, the people rejoice: but when the wicked beareth rule, the people mourn" *(Proverbs 29:2 KJV).*

Instead King David displayed the ability to manage and administrate righteously. In the book of Acts the need arose for such anointed administration of good management: "It is not reason that we should leave the word of God, and serve tables… look ye out among you seven men of honest report, full of the Holy Ghost and wisdom, whom we may appoint over this business" *(Acts 6:2-3 KJV).*

The Keys of the Kingdom

So whether you've been the victim of someone else's greed or just your own, you'll need the strategy of the Holy Spirit to get free of it. Jesus said, "I will give you the **keys of the Kingdom** of heaven…" *(Matthew 16:19)* That means we've been given access and legal entry. Notice the plural of key. Jesus used the word "keys." We have more than one entry point. There's more than one way to unlock what God has given us. Jesus also said, "The secret of the kingdom of God has been given to you…" *(Mark 4:11)*

Consider if my own house remained locked to me, then all of my possessions would be withheld and I would not be able to benefit from them. **God on the other hand wants us to have FULL ACCESS to His house and to benefit from His Kingdom here and now.**

Sound management that helps eliminate the chaos in our lives is just one major benefit of the Kingdom.

❖

CHAPTER 12

Good Management is our Key to Success

Nothing can unlock a crisis like good management can. Bad management on the other hand only expedites a crisis. We've already mentioned in our last chapter that greed and mismanagement are the root causes of most of our problems. And most of us know what a crisis looks like, but what does *sound management* look like?

What Good Management Looks Like

According to his book, "Overcoming Crisis," Myles Munroe sights management as the number one key of God's Kingdom: "Management is the effective, efficient, correct and timely use of another person's property and resources for the purpose for which they were delegated with a view to producing the expected added value" (Munroe 39).

Defined

Management can be defined by such words as: *responsibility, administration, running, managing, organisation; charge, care, direction, leadership, control, governing, governance, ruling, command, superintendence, supervision, overseeing, conduct, handling, guidance, operation.* For example: "Business improved under the management of new owners."

Every individual on this planet is a manager of something. This is what we have been designed for: "When the Lord God made the earth and filled it up with resources, the very next thing He had to do was to make a manager to take care of it. Men and women were given dominion over the earth's resources. *(Notice, however, that they were not given dominion over each other. God was still in charge of the people He had created)*" (Munroe 40).

What Poor Management Looks Like

Poor management can apply to very mundane things. For example if you over eat, you gain weight and can seriously compromise your health. Likewise, the job you keep turning up late for, will eventually hang in the balance and the relationships you don't look after will be in jeopardy.

It's all down to management. Good or bad. True management will always protect what has been placed in its oversight. Marriages that are left to ruin will fall apart. Children that are not nurtured will run wild. *Everything* in life requires right management for it to thrive and succeed: business, family, health, faith and so on.

Time is not wasted on good management and neither is the resources; notice that hoarding is not considered managing. For example you can hoard and neglect at the same time. Those who manage money invest it; they don't neglect *(or bury)* it! Why? Because money makes money. Money that's buried can't earn interest. On the other hand, money that's correctly managed can increase while you sleep! Just as seeds sown in a farmer's field, still germinate and grow while he's sleeping.

There is no Substitute for Training

Education is so vital, correct knowledge of how to use something enables us to manage it correctly. People specialise in certain things, because they want to manage them properly. Experts exist in almost every field imaginable. We educate ourselves in order to excel in managing specific areas of life. Whether we are managing money in the bank, the stock exchange or managing patients in a hospital, it all comes down to skilful management.

It stands to reason then, that whether we're raising wild horses or educating our own children, we must have the correct know-how in order to manage our affairs properly - regardless. This applies not least to the Body of Christ, where saints must be trained and equipped for works of service *(Ephesians 4:12).*

No one is exempt from the process of training. Who wants to remain a novice? "My people are destroyed for lack of knowledge..." "My people are ruined because they don't know what's right or true. Because you've turned your back on knowledge, I've turned my back on you..." *(Hosea 4:6 KJV; MSG)*

Willingness and obedience don't trump training. My six-year-old daughter might want to be a teacher or a dentist one day, but without *proper training,* I'd never let her near my mouth, no matter how much I love her! **There is no substitute for training!** And if we are faithful with little, God will make us faithful over much.

According to the Merriam-Webster online dictionary, *sound management* is defined as: "the act or skill of controlling and making decisions..." Other descriptions include: "handling, oversight, regulation, keeping, protection, safekeeping, trust, custody and stewardship."

Which raises the valid question: "Are we just stewards or are we owners?"

Ownership vs. Delegated Stewardship

God gives us the ability to be good managers and to be good stewards of what belongs to Him. Stewards are not owners - but trusted managers of what is placed in their care. **It all belongs to God.** In Psalm 115:16 it states:

The heaven of heavens is for God, but he put us in charge of the earth (MSG).

Another translation reads:

The heaven, even the heavens, are the Lord's: but the earth hath he given to the children of men (KJV).

However in both the New and Old Testament it clearly states that ownership belongs to God:

The earth is the Lord's, and everything in it.
(1 Corinthians 10:26)

The earth is the Lord's, and the fulness thereof; the world, and they that dwell therein.
(Psalm 24:1 KJV)

Authority to Manage

Our role here is to govern, rule and exercise delegated authority to manage everything placed under our care. Basically we are anointed managers, for anointed prosperity on every level.

Again in his book "Overcoming Crisis," Myles Munroe states: "He delegated the management of His creation to the human race and He calls us to account." Therefore it's clear that we are going to have to give account to God for how we managed: "...His money, His time, His gifts, His talents, His resources," including: "the house... the apartment... the car... and more" (Munroe 44).

This means that we are not in a position to claim ownership of anything, especially since "the earth is the Lord's and EVERYTHING in it!" Management is another word for stewardship, which involves accountability and requires responsibility.

Ownership involves possession, rights and title. Where stewardship involves the responsible planning and management of resources. And the concepts of stewardship can be applied to the environment, economics, health, property, information, technology and so on. God can place His stewards in all realms. Even in the scientific arena.

Joseph's Excellent Stewardship

Joseph is another perfect example of good stewardship. Like David he did not stockpile for personal gain, but for the wider distribution and welfare of others. Through wise management and stewardship, vast resources were gathered - which involved complex logistical strategy, skilful planning and organisation. What was not squandered in a time of plenty, effectively saved lives in a time of crisis.

On the contrary, the rich man mentioned in Luke 12:16-20 stockpiled for himself - Joseph stockpiled for others. Both required years of sound management, skill and hard work - yet one was selfish - the other was service. Ultimately we are caretakers and distributers of God's resources, on this earth. When we fulfil our role of being managers and stewards - as efficiently as Joseph - then everyone benefits and **everyone is elevated above the crisis.**

Fatal Mismanagement

Another example from more recent times, of mismanagement, is the unfortunate capsizing/sinking of the cruise ship, Costa Concordia *(January 13th 2012)*, just off the coast of "Isola del Giglio" on the western coast of Italy *(northwest of Rome)*. As someone who was living in Italy at the time this occurred, I can avouch for the fact that this event never left the headlines, and for months was the major talking point in most bars and cafés!

So what was the underlying problem? The courts decided that it was due to the *reckless mismanagement* of Captain Francesco Schettino who was eventually sentenced *(February 11, 2015, after a 19-month trial)* to 16 years in prison *(ten years for manslaughter, five years for causing the shipwreck, and one year for abandoning his passengers).*

Although I must add here, that there was also some speculation at the time to suggest that Schettino became a convenient fall guy for the Cruise Company "Costa Cruises," *(who did eventually disassociate themselves from him!)* To make matters worse, he was described as "Italy's most hated man," by the tabloid press and by the end of his trial, Schettino indicated that he'd spent three years, "in a media meat grinder."

Fact: Prior to the trial, the chairman of Costa Cruises, put the blame on Captain Schettino and terminated his employment in 2012. The company declined to pay for his legal defence, and eventually became a *co-plaintiff* in the trial against him.

Fact: In 2016 he appealed his sentence, but courts in Florence upheld it. The original judge ruled: "his *recklessness* was to blame for the fate of the giant ship" *(Guardian).*

The Result of Mismanagement

This was a very unfortunate incident. His case will no doubt go to appeal yet again *(according to some tabloids)*; nevertheless, at the time of this writing, things just don't improve for Captain Schettino!

In fact the order to abandon ship was not issued until *over an hour* after the initial impact. Although international maritime law requires all passengers to be evacuated within 30 minutes of an order to abandon ship, the evacuation of *Costa Concordia* took over **six hours** and not all passengers were evacuated, sadly **32 people in total lost their lives.**

He was accused of multiple manslaughter, for causing a shipwreck, for abandoning the vessel and for failing to contact the authorities when the accident happened.

He was further accused of lying during the trial, as well as in public interviews prior to trial. Prosecutor Stefano Pizza indicated that **"The captain's duty to be the last person off the ship is not just an obligation dictated by ancient maritime rules, it is also a legal obligation intended to limit the damage to those on the ship."**

Good Managers don't Issue Poor Excuses

However regarding his dry and early departure off of the vessel, Schettino's incredulous explanation was that he had, *"slipped off the ship when it capsized and he had fallen into a lifeboat!"* The newspapers helped to fuel disbelief and undermine the credibility of this account, based on pictures of him eating in restaurants shortly afterwards, while the saga continued to unfold, while others were still trapped.

The moral of this story is this: when we put ourselves first and everyone else last, we violate our role as managers and caretakers.

Now even if this Captain had been ruled innocent at trial, this situation would still have remained a tragedy for *all* involved. No one emerged a winner from this crisis and nobody was elevated. Multiple cases of mismanagement were to blame. **Regardless of any scapegoat theory - mismanagement was at the core of this crisis.**

Don't Abandon Ship

We have a lot to learn from this story. And I use this example for more than one reason. **I want to say to my colleagues in leadership - don't jump ship when the going gets tough!** I know that austerity measures are still being felt here in Europe *(at the time of writing this book - 2016)* and entire congregations are finding it hard to find employment, an extremely tough environment for many pastors, who are losing most of their best people to greener pastures elsewhere!

Entire congregations are suffering, as people - including their pastors - are jumping ship and leaving with little warning, in hope of finding work.

On a human level I understand this. Having a growing family myself, I can totally appreciate how tough things can get. But this is where our training comes in. This is when we must stand, like Paul urged the believers in Ephesus: *"...***stand your ground...** *having done all* [the crisis demands], *to* **stand [firmly in your place]"** *(Ephesians 6:13 AMP).*

*Be prepared. You're up against far more than you can handle on your own. Take all the help you can get, every weapon God has issued, so that when it's all over but the shouting you'll **still be on your feet** (MSG).*

Where's Your Rightful Place?

The question we need to be asking is this: "Where did God call me to live in the first place?" If you're going to, "...stand firmly in *your* place," you need to know where *your* place is! **The anointing is in our lives for the hard stuff!** If we are called somewhere specifically, there is always grace and the gift of faith to sustain us there. If not, then I venture to say, that you were never called there in the first place. If greed on the other hand polluted your vision, nothing can sustain the house that's built on sand!

Matthew 6:24 clearly says:

Ye cannot serve God and mammon (KJV).

Other translations say:

You must choose one or the other (VOICE).

Adoration of one feeds contempt for the other. You can't worship God and Money both (MSG).

For example, I was informed the other day of a particular pastor, here in Italy who jumped ship *(without any warning, explanation or farewell)* because he thought his church was sinking! He just got up and left! "But what about his congregation?" I hear you ask. Yes indeed, what about them! As leaders we are responsible before God, if we cause irreversible damage in other people's lives. Either God called him to shepherd the flock or He didn't.

No shepherd would abandon his sheep to the elements or to the dangers of wild predators, without involving other shepherds to take care of them.

Sadly no infrastructure whatsoever was put in place to take care of those dear people or even help them transition into other local churches. They were simply abandoned to a spiritual vacuum; perhaps we can all agree, this was not the will of God.

Self-elevation vs. Corporate-elevation

So pastors *(like any good captain)*, I urge you to stand your ground and be the *last* to abandon ship. We are accountable before God and we cannot blame the people. And if God directs you to leave, **He would never instruct you to just abandon your people without a strategy to elevate them above the crisis.**

As with Joseph, the call of God on our lives as leaders is not for *self-elevation* but for *corporate-elevation*. We are here to get behind and lift others up, to get them through the crisis. And this is Jesus' description of a crisis: "In the world you have tribulation *and* trials *and* distress *and* frustration..." *(John 16:33 AMP)*

If however, we rescue ourselves at the *expense* of others, this is not Christ like. Jesus rescued others - at the *expense* of Himself.

Having the right Motives

In the context that we lay down our very lives to serve Christ, then the saying: "The gospel is free, but it's not cheap," is correct. But there are those who actually want to make financial gains from preaching the gospel! I would say however, be careful. Instead think of Joseph, who was second in command only to Pharaoh - in all of Egypt and still did not hoard and amass wealth or success for himself *(this is not what the gifts and call of God are all about).*

Paul the apostle clearly warned about wrong motives and those who, **"...think that godliness is a means to financial gain."** He went on instead to say that, "...godliness with contentment is great gain" *(1 Timothy 6:5-8).*

Those who jump ship, simply signed up for the wrong reasons: "I consider everything a loss because of the surpassing worth of knowing Christ Jesus my Lord, for whose sake I have lost all things. I consider them garbage, that I may gain Christ" *(Philippians 3:8).* This is the true context of *gaining* from the gospel and any hidden greed is always sorely disappointed!

What does Accountability Look Like?

We have received the mandate to manage. To be honourable stewards, who faithfully administrate God's affairs, by the Holy Spirit, here on earth as it is in heaven. In short accountability looks like this:

To one servant who had been faithful it was said, *"Well done, good and faithful servant! You have been faithful with a few things; I will put you in charge of many things. Come and share your master's happiness!"* But to the unfaithful servant it was said, *"You wicked, lazy servant! ...throw that worthless servant outside, into the darkness, where there will be weeping and gnashing of teeth" (Matthew 25:21-30).*

Seventh Pillar

MONEY

❖

CHAPTER 13

God's Financial Plan

This final *(seventh)* pillar does not really function as it should but God wants to provide for His Church so that it can do everything it is called to do, something that requires both faith and commitment, but most of all finance. Therefore, teaching on tithing and sacrificial giving should be available to each member.

The Truth about Tithing

I heard a very prominent preacher recently on TV telling his congregation, "The devil can only operate in what you don't know, and that is why I must keep teaching on money, tithing, offering and giving. You cannot afford to remain ignorant and I must keep you informed so that the devil cannot use your ignorance."

I found his rather blunt statements interesting in reference to John 8:32, which says, "You will know the truth, and the truth will set you free."

The entrance and unfolding of Your words give light; their unfolding gives understanding (discernment and comprehension)...

(Psalm 119:130 AMP)

Obviously the emphasis here is on the word *to know* because without the *knowledge* of truth, that same truth cannot affect us. Therefore it can only be the truth that we *know* personally *(by revelation)* that can set us free. In fact our personal and individual knowledge of the truth is so crucial, that it keeps the enemy working tirelessly to keep us ignorant of the truth or at best, to distort it.

And in that context, I must agree with my fellow preacher; we do indeed have a responsibility to keep heralding *truth* - over and over again - in order to keep ignorance at bay. We have a responsibility to preach with the Spirit of revelation and not just *information* so that people can really *receive* the truth. In addition, any teacher will tell you: *the art of teaching is repetition!*

Tithing in this Culture of Greed

Tithing and giving in general are fundamental to our faith. And it's important for every church member to understand that God alone is our source and supply, our provider who is generous, able and willing to bless us financially. Jesus said plainly in Luke 6:38, "Give and it will be given to you." In other words, God meets our needs, when we meet the needs of others: "Whoever sows generously will reap generously" *(2 Corinthians 9:6).*

No church member should ever feel that they have been exploited or coerced into giving money. It must be voluntary. There must be understanding, faith and revelation that God will bless and help us in every way, including the financial realm. Therefore biblical teaching about tithing and giving is not just empty words, but a precious revelation that we must nurture and keep alive in this *culture of greed!*

When we as believers understand our service in this area, financial blessings are then released over both our personal lives and that of our families, ministries and churches.

Everybody must be Involved

Sometimes I've heard pastors say out of frustration: "What we need are just three or four millionaires to pay our bills." Alternatively, "Where are all the businessmen?" But how wrong this is! Three millionaires are *not* necessary. First what is necessary is *faith* in the pastor's heart. Second we need correct teaching that builds *faith* in the people, which results in commitment. Furthermore it was never intended that a few members should carry the whole financial burden; everyone should share the weight.

God wants *everyone* to love Him. As Ulf Ekman once said, "*Everyone* should praise Him. *All* should be intercessors. *All* should go out with the gospel and all should be givers. This gives strength to a believer's ministry. God does not only want specialists whom we can admire. He seeks an *entire* group who can rise up, pay the price of commitment and walk with Him. Then great power is released."

He goes on to say, "God wants *everyone* to give to His work: 'Each man should give what he has decided in his heart to give.' God expects *every* active believer to be a giver" (Ekman, The Church of the Living God 101).

Instigated by God

What we need to perceive properly is that God, not by man, instigated tithing. Even before the Law, Abraham and Jacob gave a tenth of everything *(Genesis 14:20, 28:22)*. The principle of tithing is found throughout the bible. Jesus spoke about it in Matthew 23:23, where He emphasised righteousness and compassion, but **tithing was not to be exempt. You should not do one thing and overlook the other.**

The book of Hebrews also speaks about tithing *(Hebrews 7:2-9)*. In Malachi 3:6-12, God emphasised that a tenth belongs to Him and that it should be brought into the storehouse. The storehouse can be any Christian church, ministry or organisation where one receives food and nourishment.

God instructs that we Test Him

Therefore ten percent of our income belongs to God, which simply means that **we manage better on 90 percent with God's blessings, than on 100 percent without God's blessing!** Why? Because when we do not give our tithe, we are robbing God of something that belongs to Him; the tenth does not belong to us, it belongs to God.

Giving a tenth to God means that we are surrendering, sanctifying and circumcising our income so that we can safely stand in His covenant where we can count on His blessings; only then is heaven open over us: "'Bring the whole tithe into the storehouse, that there may be food in my house. Test me in this,' says the Lord Almighty, 'and see if I will not throw open the floodgates of heaven and pour out so much blessing that you will not have room enough for it'" *(Malachi 3:10).*

Tithing puts us in a position of protection and blessing. It is God's perfect Financial Plan! Why would He create structure in everything else but leave the subject of money to our random or individual discretion?

His Kingdom and His Body are meant to be in complete order, with no chaos and no anarchy. His perfect plan for our well-being includes tithing. Once we accept this, the easier we make it for ourselves! Because our heart is always where our treasure is, and surely our hearts belong to God. Tithing is just our opportunity to prove it; where we demonstrate our faithfulness and commitment to Him in every single area of our lives, including our money!

Seed Sowing doesn't Trump Tithing

God has destined us all to be *seed sowers,* from Eden right until now but before we get into that, first it must be said that **all giving must be preceded by the tithe,** because seed sowing does not cancel out or trump the need to tithe. In fact tithing must always come before giving *(seed sowing).* Tithing is the foundation of all seed sowing. If your seed does not bring you a harvest, check your tithe, because you can't forget to tithe *(your seed can't bypass your tithe)*.

Failing to be faithful with your tithe will hinder your seed. **Make sure you tithe as a priority and then follow with your seed;** be careful to sow plentiful seed! But don't waste your precious seed by failing to tithe first.

Tithing is the Foundation of Spiritual Blessing

Notice in Malachi that tithes and offerings come together, but one precedes the other. The tithe comes first, then the seed, then the harvest. This is God's order. In other words, to sow and expect a harvest without first tithing, will make your seed ineffective. Tithing is the foundation of spiritual blessing. As with all architecture, the simple rule is this: no foundation, no building, *(unless you're building a tent!)*

> *Will a man rob or defraud God? Yet you rob and defraud Me. But you say, In what way do we rob or defraud You? [You have withheld your] tithes and offerings. You are cursed with the curse, for you are robbing Me...*
> *(Malachi 3:8-9 AMP)*

Once you have settled this about tithing in your heart then all is set and in place. **But neither is tithing alone enough in itself** *(there is more than one principle about money).* Once you have tithed then your seeds must be sown and then you must have **a lifestyle of constant giving** *(true living is in our giving).*

Many want to Give like Heaven but Live like Hell!

> *God, your God, is the God of all gods, he's the Master of all masters, a God immense and powerful and awesome.*

*He doesn't play favourites, **takes no bribes,** makes sure
orphans and widows are treated fairly, takes loving care of
foreigners by seeing that they get food and clothing.*
                                        (Deuteronomy 10:17 MSG)

Lifestyle is very important. Because some people treat
the tithe like they can use it to pay God off! God can't be
bribed or bought. **Too many people think that they can give
like heaven and live like hell,** when tithing should be the
response of our faith in God.

Odd Fact: Not many people are aware that even **John
Lennon** used to believe in tithing! And would tithe ten
percent of his *entire* income, *(to different causes, as he believed
it was the best way to save the world)*. He revealed this in an
interview back in 1980, when he announced: **"Anybody I
want to save will be helped through our tithing, which is
ten percent of whatever we earn."**

Tithing by Faith before and after the Law

Clearly, tithing alone is not enough, *(on its own merits)*.
Certainly in the New Covenant, like all else, **tithing must be
an act of faith and not law.** We know that Abraham's tithing
for instance was free of the law, because he gave a tenth *(tithe
means ten)*, 400 years **before the law** *(Genesis 14:20)*. We give
our tenth by faith because we come **after the law!**

Now I don't want to risk oversimplifying this, but those
worshiping Mammon today *(the spirit of money)*, fiercely
defend their right *not* to tithe *(using the law as their main
argument)*. How then can they rationalize Abraham's tithing,
which was completely **untouched** by the law?

If Abraham could tithe by faith then, we certainly can tithe by faith now! In fact Romans 10:17 in the King James Version says, "Whatsoever is not of faith is sin..." Other translations read: "Any action not consistent with faith is sin" *(VOICE)*; "If the way you live isn't consistent with what you believe, then its wrong" *(MSG)*. Therefore we have no business doing *anything* without faith, including tithing!

Jesus: The New Covenant

For the sake of argument about whether tithing is relevant to the New Testament or not, let's turn to Luke 11:42 where Jesus Himself is speaking and encouraging tithing:

*Woe to you Pharisees, because you give God a tenth of your mint, rue and all other kinds of garden herbs, but you neglect justice and the love of God. You should have practiced the latter **without leaving the former undone**... (see also Matthew 23:23)*

Jesus said, **"...you should not have left the former [referring to the tithe] undone."** Some people however, try and discount this; by saying that Jesus was in the Old Covenant, therefore everything that He taught was Old Covenant! Yes Jesus may have lived in the Old Covenant but He was not *under* the Old Covenant. Jesus fulfilled *(ratified)* the Old and brought *(was the mediator)* of the New; but more than that - **HE WAS THE NEW COVENANT!**

We know this because He said, "'This is my body, which is for you...' In the same way, after supper he took the cup, saying, **'This cup IS THE NEW COVENANT IN MY BLOOD...'"** *(1 Corinthians 11:24-25 - see also Hebrews 7:22; 8:6; 9:15; 12:24).*

Giving is Releasing and the First Principle of Increase

One person gives freely, yet gains even more; another withholds unduly, but comes to poverty. A generous person will prosper; whoever refreshes others will be refreshed. People curse the one who hoards grain, but they pray God's blessing on the one who is willing to sell.

(Proverbs 11:24-26)

With God, *releasing* is the first principle of increase but with man of course, it is the exact opposite! The natural man enjoys *hoarding* and *holding onto* in order to have plenty. But if we read the scripture in the Message Bible it says: "The world of the generous gets larger and larger; the world of the stingy gets smaller and smaller. The one who blesses others is abundantly blessed; those who help others are helped."

The message here is clear, that in God's economy it's the *generous* that gain the richest returns, *(so that they can give again and give more)*. Whereas those who hoard-greedily, *reduce* themselves to their own limitations *(and **decrease** in value)*. One operates in the blessing; the other operates in the curse.

So let each one give as he purposes in his heart, not grudgingly or of necessity; for God loves a cheerful giver. And God is able to make all grace abound toward you, that you, having all sufficiency in all things, have an abundance for every good work.

(2 Corinthians 9:7 NKJV)

As it is written, "He has dispersed abroad, He has given to the poor; His righteousness remains forever." Now

181

*may He who supplies seed to the sower, and bread for food, supply and **multiply the seed you have sown** and increase the fruits of your righteousness, while you are enriched in everything for all liberality, which causes thanks giving through us to God.*

(2 Corinthians 9:9-11 NKJV)

Seeds must be Sown before they can Multiply

Notice how it says, "...multiply the seed you have sown," using the past tense to imply that only the seed that *has been sown* can be multiplied. Seed that has not been sown yet cannot bring a harvest, the same way that seeds in a box cannot grow until they have been planted!

Pastor Ulf Ekman said, "Whether you sow your time, your money or something else, you will always reap the same thing that you sow, this is how it works in the natural: parsley seed does not produce carrots. It is impossible. What you put in the ground is exactly what comes up" (Ekman, Financial Freedom 113-114).

Another facet of this law is that some crops grow quickly, while others take more time. This can be both good and bad. The person who plants an olive tree seldom lives long enough to pick an olive from the same tree. **In this case it is the next generations that will reap what the previous one has planted.** Certain things bring long-term results, while other things produce a quick, but un-enduring return.

When you plant or sow something, it is better to find a seed that continues to produce fruit for a long period of time. For example, we will benefit more from the seed of an apple tree than from the seed of a radish. God has provided us with long-term areas in which to sow and He will show us exactly what they are.

The Law of Sowing and Reaping

Paul tells us that he who sows sparingly will also reap sparingly. But to encourage us, he also promises: "And God is able to make all grace abound toward you, that you, always having all sufficiency in all things, may have an abundance for every good work" *(2 Corinthians 9:8 NKJV)*. Here, God is saying that **He is the giver and we are the sowers. He supplies seed to the sower and bread for food. If we dare to place ourselves at His disposal and begin to give, this law will come into operation.**

We need to remember two important laws: **the law of sowing and reaping and the law of faith.** We must always walk in faith, and to exercise faith by beginning to sow what little seed we have. Taking just one step of faith at a time, especially when we have very little to give, or sow.

We must begin by doing something, if this law is to function for us. At a time of need it is easy to think that we ought to hold on to what we have. The mentality of the world says, "Keep what you have. Don't let anyone else have it." However, the Kingdom of God says the opposite!

Giving is Obedience

This law of sowing and reaping works. If we dare to test it, God will give us more blessings than we have room to contain. We must make a *quality* decision to always do what God tells us to do. Every time we wonder if we can afford it, we are asking our chequebook for permission! If God says yes and our chequebook says no, do it anyway. On the other hand we should not do anything if God says no, even if your chequebook says yes! **We must be led by the Holy Spirit and not by our bank balance!**

If God exhorts us to sow into a particular project, we must not delay. **When the Holy Spirit speaks, we should be prepared to sow within a second's notice.** This will bring us out of financial bondage and into freedom, where God wants every one of us to be. If we lack money at the moment, God will provide it. There is no greater satisfaction than to give to the work of God. It involves being independent of the world and having the freedom to act and do what God has told us to do.

When Paul exhorts the Corinthians to contribute to the collection for the poor in Jerusalem, he uses the substitutionary death of Jesus as a motivation for them to give. According to Paul, the reason they should give is because Christ Jesus Himself became poor so that, through His poverty, they might become rich *(2 Corinthians 8:9-14)*.

And he shall be like a tree firmly planted [and tended] by the streams of water, ready to bring forth its fruit in its season; its leaf also shall not fade or wither; and everything he does shall prosper [and come to maturity].

(Psalm 1:3 AMP)

❖

CHAPTER 14

Get in Line
for a Spiritual Harvest

We must **sow our precious seed into good soil and never sow under pressure.** God is faithful to speak to us and to direct us, thus enabling us to **give with joy.** Also we must avoid giving just random sums. Instead we must always ask God how much we are to give, because compulsive giving is emotionally driven, not faith or Holy Spirit inspired.

Other seed fell in rich earth and produced a bumper crop.
(See Luke 8:4-15 MSG)

The devil does not want believers to be generous. If he can't stop our generosity, he'll seek to divert it, so that we contribute to the wrong things. If we sow into things that are not approved by God, the devil has managed to channel our money down a blind alley and prevented it from bearing fruit.

We should do nothing out of routine or religious duty, **but let it flow out as a result of our relationship with the Lord.** In this way, we will be actively involved in what God is doing.

Motives and Good Intentions

Similarly, we **should not allow threats or flattery to motivate our giving, as this is not the leading of the Holy Spirit** either. As soon as we feel under pressure to give, we must stop immediately. This is not the correct motivation for giving - and it's the "motivation" for giving that is the most critical issue. "If the willingness is there, the gift is acceptable according to what one has, not according to what one does not have" *(2 Corinthians 8:12)*. God does not consider the amount of money given; **He looks at the motive behind the giving.**

Paul wanted to remind the believers in Corinth of their previous decision. Like the rest of us, they had a tendency to act on impulse and then go home and forget all about it. Now, a year later, Paul was writing to remind them of their decision. He said, "Now finish the work, so that your eager willingness to do it may be matched by your completion of it, according to your means" *(2 Corinthians 8:11)*.

So here's what I think: The best thing you can do right now is to finish what you started last year and not let those good intentions grow stale, your heart's been in the *right place all along. You've got what it takes to finish it up, so go to it. Once the commitment is clear, you do what you can, not what you can't. **The heart regulates the hands**...*

(*2 Corinthians 8:10-12 MSG*)

We must prove that we are willing to carry out our decisions. **God considers the promises that we make to be sacred and precious.** Just as His promises are precious to us, He wants the promises that we make to be equally precious, holy and reliable. Most ministries I know, could wall paper their offices, with all the unfulfilled pledges they've received over the years.

God is merciful. He fully understands our situation and will never condemn us. He sees our goodwill and intentions. But we should make sure that we do not forget what we have promised.

Releasing seed by Faith not Coercion

There are two important sides to this issue: on the one hand, we must be sure to keep our promises and on the other hand, we must avoid getting into legalistic bondage, by letting others force us into making wrong decisions and doing things we would otherwise never do, (*coercion: forcing people to act involuntarily*).

God has established a financial plan for His Kingdom and it involves us giving *voluntarily* to His work. **This is a ministry to the Lord, which is no less holy than praise and worship.** One thing I regret over the years is a lack of sowing, where the future harvests could have been reaped from past seed. This of course was before I received revelation on **financial increase.**

The Church is caught up with how to get more than anything else and mostly misunderstand the teaching that is given through great servants of God. Instead people use God or the ways of God in order to furbish their own desires rather than the desires of His Kingdom.

We must see that **true prosperity is more about giving than getting.** Having said that of course we need to reap the blessings to be able to give in the first place, but the harvest cannot come without the seed being planted. I believe that there are literally millions of people suffering right now because we are not giving, not as we should!

Also I can see that there are certain *categories* within the Church: some give and do not expect anything back - others give but don't give into good soil *(failing to be led by the Holy Spirit)*. Then there are those who give regularly and faithfully tithe; we can read testimonies where debts are being wiped off, salaries increased or substantial inheritances left behind. However this still seems to me to be the minority, rather than the majority!

Giving that's Inspired by the Holy Spirit

It's also important to state that God by the Holy Spirit will show you the fields to sow into and note: the **fields are always someone else's!** Yes you can sow into your own soil, obviously a farmer doesn't sow in someone else's field but into his own field but we still must remember that in the Kingdom of God, **a seed is something that we do for others that improves their welfare or increases them personally and makes their life easier.**

This can be done in a variety of ways. For example giving into certain ministries, who are helping others, can make your seed go further and reach more people. Ultimately our seed ministers and refreshes others, because giving is a ministry in itself.

Our harvests are the seeds of another's field; this is God's way of establishing. **You cannot establish unless you help someone else establish first!** You might say, like the world says, "Let me establish, have what I need first and then... perhaps, I will help someone else." The problem with this concept is that this type of self-establishing never ends. "MORE, ME & I," are always first! Self and the flesh life are always greedy and needy. But let me make it clear. **God wants us to *release* our seed to invest in the harvest field.**

The results of all this will be twofold:

- There will be a spiritual reaction: **salvation**

- Prosperity will be manifest: **spiritual and natural wellbeing**

In other words, the Body of Christ will see growth in the establishing of the Church, with the finances to do the work of the ministry. And the people of God will be blessed in *everything* they do.

Let's look at Acts 2:42-47,

> *They devoted themselves to the apostles' teaching and to the fellowship, to the breaking of bread and to prayer. Everyone was filled with awe, and many wonders and miraculous signs were done by the apostles.*
>
> ***All the believers were together and had everything in common. Selling their possessions and goods, they gave to anyone as he had need.*** *Every day they continued to meet together in the temple courts. They broke bread in their homes and ate together with glad and sincere hearts, praising God and enjoying the favour of all the people. And the Lord added to their number daily those who were being saved.*

My belief is that if we take seriously, Kingdom management *(for anointed prosperity)* this will not only bring a tremendous outpouring of the blessings of God but would also release the financial needs to the ministers of the gospel. **The end result would be revival!**

We pray for an outpouring, but **perhaps God is waiting for us to pour out our wealth to set in motion a sea of abundance** where blessings and miracles would be on the lips of every believer instead of just the few! Prosperity is not just for the minority, while everyone else is jealous - on the outside looking in - no!

If we *all* operate the way God stipulates in His Word, there is more than enough to go around; it is His plan that *everyone* can prosper. This well known little motto is very true indeed: **"The Word works for those who work it!"** *(see Matthew 13:3-23; Mark 4:2-20)*

❖

Bibliography

- Bounds, E.M. The Reality of Prayer. Copyright © 2014. Published by CreateSpace Independent Publishing Platform.

- Brown, Michael. Joseph Prince gets it right and wrong on the Day of Atonement. Copyright © 2016. Published by Charisma Media, www.charismamedia.com.

- Ekman, Ulf. Financial Freedom. Copyright © 1989. Published by Word of Life Publications. Printed in Sweden.

- Ekman, Ulf. The Church of the Living God. Copyright © 1994. Published by Word of Life Publications. Printed in Sweden.

- Gordon, Bob. Understanding the Way. Copyright © 1987. Published by Marshall and Scott. Printed in UK.

- Hamon, Bill. Apostles, Prophets and the Coming Moves of God. Copyright © 1997. Published by Destiny Image Publishers, Inc. Printed in USA.

- Hayford, Jack. Prayer is Invading the Impossible. Copyright © 2002. Published by Bridge-Logos Publishing. Printed in USA.

- Munroe, Myles. Overcoming Crisis. Copyright © 2009. Published by Destiny Image. Printed in USA.

- Murdock, Mike. Wisdom for Winning. Copyright © 1988. Published by Honor Books. Printed in USA.

- Murray, Andrew. The Ministry of Intercession. Copyright © 1898. Published by James Nisbet & Co. Limited. Printed by Morrison and Gibb Limited Edinburgh.

- Strong, James. S.T.D., L.L.D. 1890. Strong's Exhaustive Concordance; Dictionaries of the Hebrew and Greek Words. e-Sword ® version 7.6.1 Copyright © 2000-2005. All Rights Reserved. Registered trade mark of Rick Meyers. Equipping Ministries Foundation. USA www.e-sword.net.

- Thompson, Robb. The Ten Critical Laws of Relationship. Copyright © 2005. Published by Family Harvest Church. Printed in USA.

Bibliography

- Scripture quotations marked NCV are taken from the New Century Version®. Copyright © 2005 by Thomas Nelson. Used by permission. All rights reserved.

- Scripture references marked NLT are taken from the Holy Bible, New Living Translation, copyright © 1996, 2004, 2007 by Tyndale House Foundation. Used by permission of Tyndale House Publishers, Inc., Carol Stream, Illinois 60188. All rights reserved.

- Scripture references marked NKJV are taken from the New King James Version. Copyright © 1982 by Thomas Nelson, 1982 by Thomas Nelson, Inc. Used by permission. All rights reserved.

- Scripture references marked VOICE are taken from The Voice™. Copyright © 2008 by Ecclesia Bible Society. Used by permission. All rights reserved.

- Scripture references marked WYC are taken from the Wycliffe Bible. Copyright © 2001 by Terence P. Noble.

- Scripture references marked YLT are taken from the Young's Literal Translation of the bible.

Drs Alan and Jennifer Pateman

Senior and Co-Apostles

Drs Alan and Jennifer Pateman, missionaries
from the UK, who at present reside in Tuscany, Italy,
and travel together as an apostolic couple. They
are the Founders of Alan Pateman World Missions,
Connecting for Excellence International Apostolic Family Network,
and LifeStyle International Christian University.
President and Vice President of
World Missions Ministries Association
and APMI Publishing/Publications.

*(Please see our website for all profile and
international information, itinerant, conferences
and graduations, etc.)*

www.AlanPatemanWorldMissions.com

❖

To Contact the Author

Please email:

Alan Pateman World Missions

Email: apostledr@alanpatemanworldmissions.com
Web: www.AlanPatemanWorldMissions.com

*Please include your prayer requests
and comments when you write.*

❖

Other Books

Media, Spiritual Gateway

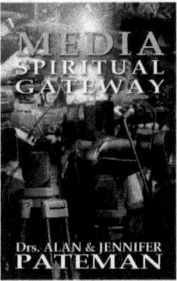

Let's face it; we live in the era of fake news! It's always existed, but never been quite so prominent. Today it's an all-out-war between fact and political fiction.

ISBN: 978-1-909132-54-2, Pages: 192,
Format: Paperback, Published: 2018
Also available in eBook format!

Millennial Myopia, From a Biblical Perspective

The standard for every generation is Jesus. However Millennial Myopia describes the trap of focusing everything on one particular generation or demographic cohort, at the exclusion and expense of all others. The Church cannot afford to make this mistake too.

ISBN: 978-1-909132-67-2, Pages: 216,
Format: Paperback, Published: 2017
Also available in eBook format!

Truth for the Journey Books

TONGUES, Our Supernatural Prayer Language

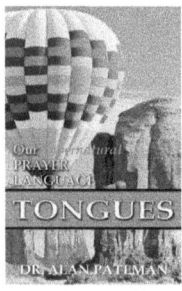

In writing to the church at Corinth, Paul encouraged them to continue the practice of speaking with other tongues in their worship of God and in their prayer lives as a means of spiritual edification. "He that speaketh in an unknown tongue edifies, charges, builds himself up like a battery."

ISBN: 978-1-909132-44-3, Pages: 144,
Format: Paperback, Published: 2016
Also available in eBook format!

WINNING by Mastering your Mind

Someone once said, "Happiness begins between your ears and your mind is the drawing room for tomorrow's circumstances..." Remember, what happens in your mind will happen in time, and therefore one of our first priorities must be mind-management.

ISBN: 978-1-909132-40-5, Pages: 136,
Format: Paperback, Published: 2017
Also available in eBook format!

Seduction & Control: Infiltrating Society & the Church

This book is a glance into the world of seduction and control, how they try to influence the Church through many powerful avenues such as the New Age, sexual education in our schools, basic entertainment; things that touch our everyday lives in order that we effectively and gradually become desensitised.

ISBN: 978-1-909132-00-9, Pages: 156
Format: Paperback, Published: 2015
Also available in eBook format!

Truth for the Journey Books

Kingdom Management for Anointed Prosperity

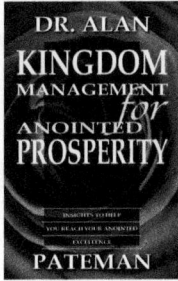

In his book, "Kingdom Management for Anointed Prosperity," Dr. Alan Pateman reveals how we can avoid living in continual crisis due to mismanagement. Life happens to all of us, but how we handle it matters most.

ISBN: 978-1-909132-34-4, Pages: 144, Format: Paperback, Published: 2015
Also available in eBook format!

Why War: A Biblical Approach to the Armour of God and Spiritual Warfare

Spiritual warfare means different things to different people, but from a biblical standpoint Ephesians 6:10-18 gives us the best biblical definition of spiritual warfare possible. We can also see how God has thoroughly equipped us for victory not just self defence!

ISBN: 978-1-909132-39-9, Pages: 180, Format: Paperback, Published: 2013
Also available in eBook format!

Forgiveness, The Key to Revival

Scripture is absolute when it comes to forgiveness. IF we forgive, THEN we are forgiven. It's that simple but no one said it was easy! Nonetheless, forgiveness can be likened to a spiritual key that unlocks spiritual doors and opportunities!

ISBN: 978-1-909132-41-2, Pages: 124, Format: Paperback, Published: 2013
Also available in eBook format!

Revival Fires - Anointed Generals
Past & Present (Part Two of Four)

Seasons might be changing but God's Word remains the same. The heart of the author is to help train, equip and be a blessing to those men and women who will be willing to fulfil their potential in ministry and be properly equipped for service.

ISBN: 978-1-909132-36-8, Pages: 142,
Format: Paperback, Published: 2012
Also available in eBook format!

Prayer, Touching the Heart of God (Part Two)

Touching the Heart of God is the very essence of prayer. Whether we are petitioning God with very specific requests or consecrating ourselves before Him and rededicating our lives - whatever the case may be – the true essence of all praying is "Touching the Heart of God."

ISBN: 978-1-909132-12-2, Pages: 180,
Format: Paperback, Published: 2012
Also available in eBook format!

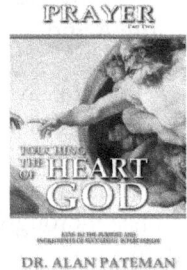

Prayer, Ingredients for Successful Intercession
(Part One)

This Book is the first of two books on Prayer. Dr. Pateman provides an exhaustive study, showcasing the vital ingredients necessary for all successful prayer. An excellent power-packed teaching tool, either for the individual or for the local church prayer group, that's eager to lay a solid foundation but don't know where to start!

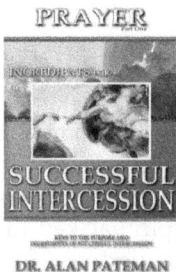

ISBN: 978-1-909132-11-5, Pages: 140,
Format: Paperback, Published: 2012
Also available in eBook format!

Truth for the Journey Books

Apostles: Can the Church Survive Without Them?

Before Jesus returns a significant increase of the anointing will be poured out on the Body of Christ, but can the Church handle such an anointing? *(Acts 5:5)* Billy Brim once said, "As much as the anointing is powerful to create, it is as powerfully destructive of evil." The fear of God will be restored with the apostolic and people will begin walking with such anointing, as we have never seen before!

ISBN: 978-1-909132-04-7, Pages: 164,
Format: Paperback, Published: 2012
Also available in eBook format!

Sexual Madness: In a Sexually Confused World

This book discusses the sensitive subject of political correctness in our world today and the growing fear of causing offence in the public arena. It also discusses the rise of homosexuality, pedophilia and all other forms of sexuality, as there are many. Including modern statistics on pornography.

ISBN: 978-1-909132-02-3, Pages: 160,
Format: Paperback, Published: 2012
Also available in eBook format!

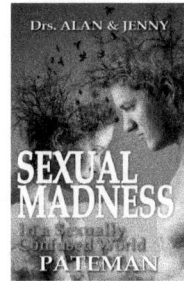

His Life is in the Blood

Blood is the trophy of every battle. The spilt blood of Jesus Christ is our trophy. It is our freedom from sin and bondage. Nothing can enter the blood-bought temples of the Holy Ghost! This book will encourage you to apply the blood of Jesus our Passover Lamb to your life, just as the children of Israel did in the Old Testament. Not merely talking or reading about it, but applying it.

ISBN: 978-1-909132-06-1, Pages: 152,
Format: Paperback, First Published: 2007
Also available in eBook format!

All Books Available

at

APMI PUBLICATIONS

Email: publications@alanpatemanworldmissions.com
*Also Available from Amazon.com
and other retail outlets.*

*If you purchased this book through Amazon.com
or other and enjoyed reading it, or perhaps one of
my other books, I would be grateful if you could
take a couple of minutes to write a Customer
Review, many thanks.*

BY DR. ALAN PATEMAN

BY DR. JENNIFER PATEMAN